Changing Places

Changing Places

Dr. Cheryl Snyder D.O.

ISBN: 197957555X
ISBN-13: 9781979575553
Library of Congress Control Number: 2018900813
San Diego, California

Contents

This book is dedicated to:
My students, you have taught me so much.
My family, you have shown me love.
My friends, you have stayed near in good times and bad.
My Lord, you made the journey possible and deserve all the glory.

Acknowledgments

A SPECIAL THANKS TO Ms. Christina Shimamoto and Mrs. Ruth Harrison, who so kindly labored with the editorial work on my manuscript. You encouraged me to press on and bring this story to others.

CHAPTER 1

Lights, Camera, Action!

A TYPICALLY QUIET, SIT-BACK-and-enjoy-your-black-coffee type of early morning in the emergency department is suddenly transformed. "Trauma code to the ER!" blasts the overhead speaker. Sirens approach. Minutes later, paramedics roll a stretcher into the emergency department. On it lies a gasping thirty-five-year-old man.

"Stab wound to his left chest," the medic reports, motioning to the knife still protruding from above the left nipple. "I guess the wife was a little angry with him today," he continues. "Cops have her in custody."

A pulsating trickle of bright red blood verifies there is still some hope.

Welcome to my dramatic life as an emergency physician. This is what I am involved in, the business of fixing broken people.

My experiences encompass the full gamut of emotions found in human life: indescribable joy that comes from being the first to greet a new life coming into this world, tearful desperation on watching life slip away from my touch into eternity despite the best that medicine has to offer, exploding anger at the intentional injustices inflicted by one human on another more vulnerable, and the unwavering gratefulness for just being a part of the drama of saving lives and helping wounded people.

For me, training for a career of blood and guts in the emergency department (ED) began even before the age of five, living within fifty miles of Hollywood. On an occasional weekend night, my parents would load their 1960s Chevy station wagon with four pajama-clad children aged three to nine and take us out for a night at the movies. As we would eat McDonald's burgers and fries under the California stars at the outdoor drive-in theater, my parents shared with us their fascination with Vincent Price thrillers. Though I regularly hid behind a blanket in the beginning, afraid of the violence, this is when I began the process of desensitization to the shocking things I would see two or three decades later. Those movies were notorious for large doses of horror-provoking visual effects, including disjointed body parts crawling on the ground and talking heads sitting alone on a table. The story of a mad scientist dressed in his bloody white lab coat proudly displaying his experimental human projects was my earliest experience with "medical research." Long before the reality of cloning, my imagination was active with the possibilities of a little applied scientific knowledge.

Storytelling was my favorite part of school as a kindergartener. Fellow students would often sit shyly in the back of the classroom during show-and-tell time, but I was quick to take center stage and share my excitement over the most recent movie thriller, complete with my own dramatized descriptions. Unfortunately, for some inexplicable reason, my teacher did not appreciate my gruesome enthusiasm, so my storytelling days in class came to an end. But it was just the beginning of my passion for incredible stories.

In those early years, I also had the opportunity to experience the ED from a patient's perspective. One late August night as a fifteen-year-old, I was awakened by a sudden intense abdominal pain. As the waves of pain increased, I concluded that this must be the way I would die. I thought I was like the people I had seen in the movies, gasping out their final words like a fish out of water. I woke up my younger sister, who slept in the upper bunk bed, and tasked her with breaking the news of my final good-byes. "Just tell Mom I think I'm dying," I said haltingly between my waves of pain and nausea. The journey downstairs to my parents' bedroom seemed a huge distance to send her in the dark, but I thought it was only right my mother should know my end was in sight. Fortunately, my sister was willing to go.

Thankfully, my mother had the wisdom to ignore my dramatic "last words" and rushed me to a nearby emergency department. Once there, I was placed beneath the cold white sheets on a gurney as I writhed in pain. My mother stood by, dabbing away tears from her eyes. The pulsating, sharp, stabbing pain caused by a kidney stone traveling through the urine-collection system of my body was thankfully not terminal and didn't continue for long. Instead, the experience became inspirational fuel, propelling me on to the career path of being a nurse. I saw my nurse as a superhero and wanted to be just like her. Whatever she gave me in my vein took away my pain, and in my eyes, it was nothing short of a miracle. The painful incident was a disguised gift of career direction. A few years later, I chose to enter a nursing program at the local community college.

After years working as a nurse in intensive care units and emergency departments, I still had a lot of curiosity about how things worked in the human body. Additionally, I had a desire to take my knowledge beyond the US borders. I started to do some volunteer work in Mexico at a location known as the Tijuana Dump. This was where the city's waste was put, and subsequently, the poor sifted through the discards to find enough to live on. I heard that a small group had formed to bring some medical care to that community.

The clinic was a small concrete one-room building without water or electricity. The needs were desperate, and sometimes someone in the community would die before we returned the next weekend, which saddened all of us. Without the advanced technology and multitude of well-trained doctors I had available in the United States, I felt limited in what I could do. I was equipped to teach basic first-aid training, which I did, using the text *Where There Is No Doctor*, conveniently translated into Spanish. The recruited local women were encouraged to develop skills to help their community. They in turn were an inspiration, and I proceeded to gain more advanced exam, diagnostic, and treatment skills. I began training and became a nurse-practitioner to better assist the underserved patients of this needy community.

As I neared completion of the nurse-practitioner program, I still felt limited in my knowledge and skills. At that time, I truly believed I was supernaturally pulled in the direction of even more study to pursue the career of emergency physician. This revelation was met with some initial resistance on my part, as I had already put so many years into my training. I had completed more than twenty-two years of education up to the master's level, and another eight years seemed monumental. I thought I was already prepared for my life dream. During my twenties, I had also completed training as a commercial pilot so I could fly into remote settings to establish clinics. I was actively flying with a group of pilots, gaining hours and experience at clinics in Mexico. However, I could not ignore this new nudge to change direction, which daily gained momentum. Something within me seemed to say this additional education was a part of my purpose on earth. Memories of the desperate people I had met as a volunteer nurse in Haiti, Honduras, and various countries in Africa provided the inspirational fuel to press on with my studies in medicine. Once these were completed, this career gave me the ability to save many desperate lives.

I had been *desensitized* to bloodied bodies long ago, thanks to the horrors of Vincent Price movies.

I had been *sensitized* to pain because of my own experiences and those of the patients I cared for.

However, as in all good dramas, somewhere the roles change. Greedy, selfish Scrooge is transformed by a dream and freely gives out Christmas gifts. The justice-serving Batman, working undercover to defend the helpless, gets corrupted by the "weaker species." The *Star Wars* hero dies, and the universe is never the same. In 2008, I found myself in a role change as well, by the transforming power of my own diagnosis. Once again, I found myself beneath cold white sheets on a gurney.

This new drama, however, did not come with a quick response to medication, as my first medical condition had. In this new role as a patient, months passed as I waited for the correct diagnosis. Delays, errors, and denial all played leading roles. The question that persisted in my mind was, Why the delays?

CHAPTER 2

When Delays Can Mean Death

My first job with urgency was at the Carl's Jr. fast-food restaurant within walking distance of my house. At the age of sixteen, I began my novice attempt at keeping people from waiting. On the starting day of my first job, with minimal training, I was assigned to fill soda cups from the drink machine. The task included marking the lid once it was placed properly to indicate whether the cup contained root beer, Coke, or Pepsi. Brown fizz was more than just brown fizz, and the customers would have to wait if I mixed them up.

It was a very busy Saturday, and I found myself low on time but high on adrenaline. Hungry customers were grumpy, and the manager was doing what she could to restore peace and dissipate the hostility. A bus rolled into the parking lot and unloaded a team of football players. I, much too prematurely, was thrust into a game of speed with the more experienced. "Left cup Pepsi, right side Coke, middle root beer," I mumbled under my breath. In an effort to quickly seal the top of the first in the line of filled soda cups, my adrenaline-enriched strength overcame the flimsy cardboard of the cup, which collapsed like an accordion. One cup after another responded to the infamous domino effect, and they toppled with what seemed like lightning speed.

Sticky brown fluid gushed all over the floor like a fire hydrant had gone awry. Orders stopped, and mouths hung open. Productivity ground to a halt as workers stuck to the floor, and the manager screamed out orders to mobilize the cleanup forces. It was mortifyingly dramatic and certainly one of the worst moments of my relatively short life. Customers waited irritably to fill their grumbling stomachs as I mopped up the disaster. There was one mitigating factor for them, however. They knew who was to blame for the wait. All eyes were on me.

Delays are not a modern problem; they have been present since the beginning of time and affect all of us. The air is still, and the temperatures seem to soar as cars screech to a stop in the morning traffic. Stop. Go. Stop. Go. More delays. This was not in our master plan, so we complain. None of us are immune. Delays come in various shapes and sizes, but they are usually as unwanted today as they were thousands of years ago. Lazarus's family would agree: "Now a man named Lazarus was sick. He was from Bethany, the village of Mary and her sister Martha…So the sisters sent word to Jesus, 'Lord, the one you love is sick.' When He heard this, Jesus said, 'This sickness will not end in death. No, it is for God's glory so that God's Son may be glorified through it.' Jesus loved Martha and her sister and Lazarus. Yet when he heard that Lazarus was sick, He stayed where He was two more days" (John 11:1–6, NIV).

Lazarus was a sick man who was well loved by friends and family. He knew the miracle worker, Jesus, so quickly word was sent for the healer to come. Delay followed. Lazarus succumbed to death, and his loved ones watched helplessly as he drew in his last breath. As one reads this story, it is easy to think, "Really, Jesus? Your good friend Lazarus was on the verge of death and you delayed? Surely there was no time to wait." In our limited understanding from earth's perspective, life just does not make sense sometimes. Miles away from the scene, Jesus gives the reason for the delay to his questioning followers: "It is for God's glory" (John 11:4, NIV).

What personal delays have left you hopeless and wondering, "Why?"

This ancient story holds wisdom for our questioning minds. It is an example of when the simple mathematical equation of one plus one does not equal two. Beyond human thoughts and possibilities, something dramatic was going to happen, but at the time, no one understood. As with my experience as a novice fast-food worker, somehow, knowing why a delay has occurred helps with the waiting, but life does not always afford us that jewel of knowledge. In my years of education, I came to recognize that the more I learned, the less I realized I actually knew about a particular subject.

Study of the microscopic world and the advent of the electron microscope opened up realms of even greater knowledge regarding the function of cells. Various organisms were identified, and their benefit to the human species grew exponentially. We know the human body has more than one hundred trillion cells, with ten times as many bacterial cells as human cells, which are critical to the health of the body. The heart pumps two thousand gallons of blood per day, and there are about sixty thousand miles of blood vessels in the human body. Just last year, neuroscientists discovered lymphatic vessels in the brain that have more than one hundred billion nerve cells. Your sneeze, which is typically invisible, can reach speeds of more than one hundred miles per hour![1]

On the other extreme of universal knowledge, the Hubble telescope just cracked the door of the galaxies. According to NASA, our galaxy, the Milky Way, has hundreds of billions of stars and enough gas and dust to make billions more stars. It is all held together by gravity. The Hubble observed a tiny patch of sky (one-tenth the diameter of the moon) for one million seconds (11.6 days) and found approximately ten thousand galaxies of all sizes, shapes, and colors. NASA persists in believing in the Big Bang theory of the formation of the universe but can't answer what happened next, and questions persist on their web page. Did small particles slowly team up and gradually form stars, star clusters, and eventually galaxies? Or did the universe first organize as immense clumps of matter that later subdivided into galaxies?[2]

I am willing to acknowledge that I have never seen something spontaneously go from less complex to more complex, and I would not know where to begin forming a star and suspending it in the universe with the right amount of gravitational pull. Within the circle of all universal knowledge, my acumen seemed to shrink despite more years of study and experience. Perhaps, within the acceptance of this truth, I can begin to look at delays a little differently. However, it will take work.

"To wait" can be defined as "to stay in place in expectation."[3] It is the joyful excitement of waiting for a wedding day to arrive or the distressing feeling of waiting for a missing child to return home. In the past, I joined with the human rat race in seeking efficiency and minimizing wait times. Alarms, day planners, calendars, and timers kept me moving forward toward planned goals. Breakfast, lunch, and dinner engagements were scheduled months in advance to fit into an already-impacted to-do list. A synchronized clock ticking on my wrist echoed in every room at home and work. I always had a sense of what time it was and how fast time was passing. It was my job. It gave me a sense of control. This was my daily routine. This was the way I lived.

Work in a busy emergency department is the incubator for those labeled as "time freaks." As I gained experience as an ED nurse and then an ED physician, my skills at managing time also developed. The chart racks had built-in stopwatches for recording how many minutes and seconds the patients had been waiting in the room for the doctor. Every working moment was a sprint from room to room to room. In those days, the priority was always airway, breathing, and circulation problems, in that exact order. Seconds count in my specialty, and delays make the difference between life and death. Delays were not an option.

"Brain attack" is common terminology for a stroke, which occurs when the blood supply—more specifically, life-giving oxygen and sugar in the blood—is suddenly cut off, and the brain tissue malfunctions. "Time is brain" is what we know. Reasons can vary, but the presentation will be similar, depending on the part of the brain affected. Microscopically, we know there are about 22 billion neuron cells in the area of the brain typically affected by strokes. For every minute that passes without restoring blood flow, 1.9 million neuron cells die.[4] Outwardly, what we might see is that dearly loved Grandma has stopped talking and walking normally. Standard protocols are initiated for rapid response in all emergency departments in the United States to restore blood flow as soon as possible and reverse the devastating loss of neurological function. When the tissue lacking the life-giving nutrients is the heart instead of brain, the presenting complaint will be different.

"I feel like an elephant is sitting on my chest," Sam, the sixty-year-old sweaty, pale mechanic gasps out as he grabs his chest in a weak attempt to control the excruciating pain. "Time is muscle" is our mantra as the team moves into action within minutes of his arrival. His heart's blood vessels were narrowing as sticky platelets piled up on cholesterol plaques. The World Health Organization reports cardiovascular disease as the number one cause of death worldwide and includes 31 percent of deaths, more than 17.2 million per year.[5] As each second passes, thousands of irreplaceable heart cells are dying. The heart pump, which provides life-giving blood flow to all the organs of his body, is about to fail. Sam, however, is more than just a combination of body organs. He is wonderfully made. He is loved. In front of me is someone's brother, husband, father, son fighting a battle for his life. The medical team comes along, and we join the battle with him to do everything we can as fast as we can.

Time is of the essence, and as oxygen levels drop precipitously in the tissue, the heart becomes an unsynchronized bag of Jell-O. Anarchy reigns, followed by an irregular, fatal rhythm.

"All clear," shouts the emergency doctor with a quick look around the gurney to ensure the safety of her staff. Thud. One shock of 360 joules of electricity jolts Sam's heart and restores the life-giving synchronized rhythm. Life and hope have been restored as well, and speed has made the difference. More time has been given to this brother, husband, father, son…my patient.

But now, I was the patient, and time did not seem to be of the essence. It took eight months of waiting and delays to discover the true diagnosis. Cancer. My previous leading role as healer had been given to another. The silent expressions on the familiar faces of medical colleagues and their darting eyes answered my questions about the prognosis. My days were numbered because of this deadly disease. Who really knows the count?

From my first day on the job as a novice at speed through my long career as an emergency nurse and physician, I learned a lot about quickly helping other people get out of their sticky situations. But questions ruminated in my mind like a recurring nightmare, destroying my peace. Had I learned enough to get me through this life-or-death situation that I was facing? Was it possible that somewhere in the great knowledge of the universe, this delay would ultimately be for my good? Could I have minimized the delay in some way? Was there truly a greater force guiding the timing of the events of my life? Was this delay actually a part of the plan?

Dear Creator of the universe,
This new chapter of my life has left me feeling out of control. I know it is really not about delays but about control. I believe my well-planned life is ultimately subject to Your master control. I surrender it once again. Help me to believe this delay in determining my deadly diagnosis will be for my good and Your glory!
Amen.

Notes

1. Reference.com, "What are some weird or odd facts about the human body?" https://www.reference.com/science/weird-odd-human-body-20c5d1dcbca1e841?aq=cells+human+body&qo=similarQuestions.
2. "Galaxies," NASA, https://science.nasa.gov/astrophysics/focus-areas/what-are-galaxies.
3. *Merriam-Webster Online,* s.v. "wait," https://www.merriam-webster.com/dictionary/wait.
4. Jeffrey L. Saver, "Time Is Brain—Quantified," *Stroke* 37 (2005):263–66, http://stroke.ahajournals.org/content/37/1/263, doi: https://doi.org/10.1161/01.STR.0000196957.55928.ab.
5. "Cardiovascular Diseases (CVDs) Fact Sheet," World Health Organization, last revised May 2017, http://www.who.int/mediacentre/factsheets/fs317/en/.

CHAPTER 3

Detours

WHEN I REFLECT ON WHAT delays preceded my cancer diagnosis, I trace them back to detours and grace. Grace reminds me of Grace Clinic. To get to the story of Grace Clinic, I will first need to take you on a detour to many countries, starting in the United States and returning to the United States. Pack your bags!

To date, I have been fortunate enough to travel to more than forty different countries, some on more than one occasion. I always had renewed appreciation for the laws, roads, and transportation systems in the United States—even with our rush hour traffic! Though at times the trips were for leisure, the majority involved various efforts to assist with medical care for those living with very limited resources. I found joy in recognizing that my small contribution could help improve life for another in some way. Ultimately, each trip would leave me with the gift of a greater appreciation of, specifically, the American medical system.

However, emergency medicine comes face-to-face with harsh realities in America. The contrast in options available to the haves and the have nots—those who have medical insurance and those without. Granted, there are people who can afford insurance but choose not to purchase it, but by far, the greater percentage of people without insurance are those who find themselves stretched financially despite working two or three part-time jobs to support a family. Those are the cases that break our hearts, knowing our best medical care will break them financially. We see them after tragedy has struck. They are like Sam, the mechanic in the last chapter, who just didn't have enough left over at the end of the month to put out hundreds of dollars to protect himself from the potential destructive financial force that an unexpected accident, stroke, or heart attack could cause next month. Food on the table *today* for his children was far more important.

Those who present to an emergency department in the United States experiencing a life-or-death situation get attended to regardless of their ability to pay or carry an insurance card. I am grateful I do not have to curtail interventions based on finances. The bill will come later. This is not so for those living in countries without socialized medicine; patients or their families must render payment prior to the initiation of treatment, even for life-threatening conditions. What might surprise some is that the majority of people presenting to an emergency department in the United States are *not* in a life-or-death situation. For some it is an issue of discernment of severity of the problem; for others it is financial. The average person is not trained to adequately discern a true emergency and to know when it might be more appropriate to go to a private doctor or urgent care. Financially, all medical clinics will require proof of insurance or some payment up front to render services. The emergency department is the exception.

For one patient, after two months of a persistent cough, a chest x-ray revealed a suspicious mass that required a visit to a specialist. Another, after a visit to the ED, walked away with a new diagnosis of diabetes that was going to require regular lifelong and very costly medical follow-up to prevent amputation, blindness, stroke, and heart attack. That necessary care would just have to be on hold until the patient could buy insurance. Often, after a referral to an oncologist or other specialist to manage a newly diagnosed condition, I would hear, "But, Doc, I don't have insurance, and they will charge more than two hundred dollars just to see me!" Those cases broke my heart.

I WANTED TO DO MORE, BUT WHAT WAS THE SOLUTION TO THIS DESPERATE SITUATION?

After studying the Bible to better understand God's heart for the poor and needy, I felt a desire to go to one of the neediest areas at the time and teach emergency medicine. At a hospital in southern India, a new residency program was being developed for emergency doctors who had the same calling as I did. By September of 2001, now living as a single mom, I had finished preparing my two daughters, ages eight and twelve, for this adventure. We were partially packed and linguistically prepared with a few practiced Hindi greetings. We had familiarized ourselves with the basics of the Hindu religion and how it differed from Christianity. Suddenly, our life trajectory was rerouted, and plans dramatically changed.

Hijacked airplanes crashing into 110-story buildings more than three thousand miles away on September 11, 2001, mandated significant changes worldwide. As the airports of the world, including those in India, were closed to travel, my eyes were opened to the poor in my own backyard. I became aware of the needs of the more than twenty thousand uninsured people in my own community in eastern Washington—more specifically, the Benton-Franklin Counties. These were neighbors in need; almost one in six people was among the "have nots" with regard to medical insurance. Most of them also fell into the federal poverty classification based on insufficient income for the size of their families. The detour provided me with clarity of vision to see the needy faces of those nearby and not just those more distant.

These were the faces I would see in the ED, asking, "Doc, could you prescribe the cheapest antibiotic?" as they navigated the tough decisions. Should they fill their prescription, get shoes for their kids, or pay the rent? Their follow-up for a possible cancer growth would have to wait because they were behind on car payments. I was challenged by a deep stirring within my soul to do something about the plight of these precious people stuck in the maze of the US health-care system. No one should be denied necessary medical care because of their inability to pay.

But what could I do alone?

On an icy-cold Sunday in November in that needy community in eastern Washington, the answer began to take shape. During a casual meeting with a local pediatrician friend, Dr. Carol Endo, a spark of possibility ignited over our steamy cups of coffee. Bursts of brainstorming ideas to help our neighbors evolved into a steady stream of solutions. Two hours later—as my children waited patiently at the local buffet—a clinic was conceived with details jotted down on a napkin. Together we had experienced the value of medical mission trips to poor communities, and now we wanted to help the poor around us. Just a few months previously in Honduras, we had been a part of a team with Mercy Ships that was able to address hundreds of physical, emotional, and spiritual needs in just a week of service. With our new plan, we asked ourselves if it would be possible to open a free clinic in the United States where patients could be treated holistically and their medical, emotional, spiritual, and social needs met in one place.

Time was of the essence. The limitations we had faced in providing definitive care to the needy people we had treated that week in our practices were fresh in our minds. We both knew of premature deaths as a result of delayed medical care. People avoided treatment due to fear of large expenses. Each day we waited, we knew more lives would be lost because of the lack of adequate, affordable medical care. We generated a list of those who might join us in the cause.

Initial meetings were held at my home with a small group of passionate people from the community. In the same month, November 2001, the First Methodist Church in Pasco decided to dedicate storage space for a clinic. However, they needed medical personnel. We had medical personnel but needed space. It was a marriage made in heaven. The many connections coordinated by God helped us with the final selection of the name: Grace Clinic.

Our acronym, Grace, stood for God's riches at Christ's expense. His love for us was what motivated us in turn to love our neighbors. The mission was clear: "bringing Christ's love and healing to those in need." The United Way performed an assessment of community need, and decisions were made quickly, but prayers were endless. In a whirlwind of six months, we had recruited a team of volunteer doctors, dentists, nurses, and pharmacists. Local grocery stores were willing to donate food, and hospitals offered some unused medical supplies. On June 1, 2002, we opened the doors of the community's first free clinic in nine hundred square feet of recently remodeled space in a church basement, funded through generous donations of time, talents, and treasures...not to mention a yard sale at my home!

As a start-up project in a community with limited resources, it required intense work from many people, both young and old. Everyone we could think of was recruited. My daughters participated every Saturday in that church basement, setting up or taking down chairs, making coffee, handing out free food and clothing, and keeping the children of patients entertained in the childcare room while their parents were being examined in the very small exam rooms. It was a community effort that brought energy to all of us, along with lasting friendships. Small and large financial donations came from near and far. Often, recovering patients or their family members gratefully slipped a few dollars into the hand-carved donation box made by a former patient. Some even returned as volunteers to help others in need or to use their skills to assist with logistics.

In a relatively short time, I saw the miraculous delivery of a whole-person-care approach transforming our needy neighbors and also unifying our previously medically segregated community. Through various grants, such as United Way, and private donations, we were able to provide free medical care, dental care, mental health counseling, pharmaceuticals, lab services, diabetic education, specialist referral services, and spiritual health counseling by chaplains to uninsured people in my community. The food and clothing banks provided practical resources, and often, we could link patients to a variety of other social welfare services through the work of Love Inc. and the public health-department workers who volunteered at the clinic. I was astounded at how many early cancers we detected on screening and how many of those were treated successfully, giving hope back to our patients.

Ultimately, the spiritual transformation seen in the volunteer workers, the patients, and their families was our greatest reward. One patient in particular, Euladio, represented the impact of the ministry. Arriving within a month of the clinic opening, he tested our faith in God and our new ministry. He was a depressed and despairing forty-five-year-old Hispanic man, blind as a result of inadequately treated diabetes. He had one request. He wanted to see again. The cataracts in the front of his eyes were thick, and most likely, there was damage to the back of his eyes (retinas) due to his diabetes and lack of preventative care. As an emergency doctor, I was privileged to participate in those life-giving shocks to restore cardiac function to one who had no heartbeat. I knew that God could do miraculous things with and without doctors, but could He restore sight to the desperate man who sat in front of me, as recorded in the Bible? The convoluted, mazelike process of navigating the medical system is daunting enough for an experienced physician, but for an uninsured, uneducated, poor, despairing blind man…this would require a miracle.

It is said if you want to see a miracle, expect the impossible. We prayed for a miracle.

After we placed a few calls, an unexplainable series of medical appointments occurred, resulting in referrals to generous and talented specialists throughout the state of Washington, who performed the necessary complex surgeries. At our first Grace Clinic celebration, six months after opening, Euladio inspired all of us with his short journey to the speaker's podium, unassisted by his usual white cane. He gave his personal testimony of how his physical sight was restored after living in darkness for nearly a decade. His heart-wrenching story of being spiritually delivered from a time of darkness to the light of God's love through this healing process brought hope to everyone. In unity, we sang the familiar hymn:

> Amazing Grace, how sweet the sound that saved a wretch like me.
> I once was lost but now am found, was blind but now I see.

Five years and many patients later, I began sensing I was in a transition. Preparing to leave that place of miracles and friends was hard, but I knew it had developed into a self-sustaining ministry and was going to, by God's grace, thrive in the years to come. By 2007 we had provided holistic medical care to thousands of patients, had just moved into a leased, newly remodeled seven-thousand-square-foot clinic, had an established board composed of local business professionals, and were blessed with a multitude of committed volunteers and a few paid staff. The ministry had evolved into more of a primary-care model, with many patients returning for care of chronic diseases.

Grace Clinic had great promise to continue to serve the community, and it was time for me to move on to fulfill the next vision I was given. At the time of this writing, it has been more than fifteen years since that clinic opened, and it has provided more than sixty-three thousand patient visits free of charge. About fifty-five hundred were provided for medical dental and mental health services in 2017 by over three hundred volunteers that contributed in excess of seventeen thousand hours of service. More than five universities and medical schools from various states now send their trainees to the site to experience the holistic approach and learn how to better meet the needs of the medically uninsured in a community.[2]

The process of developing Grace Clinic taught me detours are not necessarily bad but in fact can be the beginning of an amazing chapter in our stories. Vision and faith improve when we look over our shoulders and see where we have traveled. If I had not been detoured away from India, I would have missed my experience with Grace Clinic.

How would this life lesson help me process my current prognosis and all the delays and detours I experienced with that diagnosis?

WHAT HAVE YOU LEARNED IN THE PROCESS OF LOOKING BACK ON YOUR LIFE AND APPRECIATING DETOURS?

"Detour ahead!"

In 2008, less than six months after leaving Grace Clinic in capable hands, I was very focused on preparing a team of emergency medicine trainers to volunteer in China for the second year in a row. My new vision was the education provided through another volunteer organization I founded, Partners for Life (PFL), which was committed to saving lives through holistic emergency medical training. Our pilot trip was to Turkey in 2006, where we taught in various emergency departments and provided disaster practice for the medical and nursing staffs. Our brief visit to Shanghai in 2007, coordinated by my friend Ruth Harrison, an English teacher, clearly demonstrated the people's interest in additional training in disaster preparedness. On that visit, we thoroughly enjoyed meeting our Chinese medical colleagues and sharing our knowledge in exchange for their mastery in traditional Chinese medicine. They were such hospitable people! We had huge banners and banquet meals welcoming us to their city as if we were famous celebrities or dignitaries. I wrote disaster scenarios and applied makeup on volunteer actors who would prompt emergency response from the medical providers. Now I was like a Hollywood director. Five local news stations covered the action of the disaster response and asked, "Why have you come to China?" My answer was simple: "To save lives."

In 2008 we received invitations from additional training sites, and I was preparing some new as well as returning volunteer participants for the journey. Just weeks before the departure, once again my life took a significant detour. Looking back over my shoulder, I could see the trail of warning signs and preparation for what was to come. Even passing the baton at Grace Clinic in October 2007 was a part of the necessary preparation. Reflecting back on the development of PFL, I can better understand the delays in my own diagnosis.

In July 2007 I transferred my own medical care to a new provider and underwent the routine annual exam. During that physical evaluation, she expressed concern about an area of thickening in my right breast, and I responded that I had fibrocystic breast disease. This is a common condition in women, resulting in "lumpy" breasts, a benign condition that will dissipate later in life when the body is not as dominated by hormonal influences. The irregularity makes it difficult to differentiate between normal lumps and anything new or suspicious on self-exams and even under the discerning fingertips of a well-trained physician. I assured her in a dismissive way, "They are always lumpy." She proceeded to order a screening mammogram and added an ultrasound of the area to just be certain. A week later I received the report: "Benign fibrocystic changes."

A few months later, in October 2007, I found the thick area to be more prominent on a self-exam. With such a recent benign report, I was not initially alarmed but began to be concerned. Certainly, I didn't have any risk for breast cancer. Not a trace of breast cancer in my family. I reviewed what the medical literature had to say about breast cancer risks [1] since it had been years since I had studied it in medical school. I seemed to be fairly immune. No alcohol intake, no postmenopausal obesity, and no one would say I lived a sedentary lifestyle! Yes, I had had my first child soon after turning thirty, had used hormonal birth control, and was currently on hormone supplementation to decrease my risk of coronary artery disease (heart attacks), but so were most of my friends. I decided to remove one of the culprits for fibrocystic changes, caffeine. Sure enough, things seemed to improve or so I thought after I stopped my green tea.

Life moved very quickly during that season of my life, and somehow, it seemed like I had been shortchanged and somehow given only twenty-three hours in a day, when everyone else was granted twenty-four. I was always on the run and coming up short on time. Looking back on that fall of 2007, this was the season I was transitioning out of my work at Grace Clinic and into the development of the work of Partners for Life, recruiting team members and responding to international and domestic e-mails multiple times a day. In addition, I had out-of-town medical conferences I needed to attend, and through it all, I continued working full-time in the emergency department. Home life was busy as a single mother of two teenagers, now fourteen and eighteen years old, as well as being a type of foster mom to a teenage Chinese exchange student who had come to live with us that year. There were plenty of tennis matches to attend, chauffeuring to do, and teen parties to prepare for in any given week. Mothers who survive the tumultuous hormonal years of life with teenage girls deserve a medal of courage. As the young women are learning to exert their independence and experiencing the intensity of their emotional roller coaster of relationships, moms can become dizzy!

In early December 2007, during another breast self-exam, the vague thickness I had noted in October had increased, and the foundation of denial was beginning to crack. Something was wrong. I scheduled an appointment with my physician later in the month, but with an unexpected increase in visitors and activities during the Christmas holiday, I made the decision to cancel it. On December 26, after a series of delays and now with the celebration behind me, I ordered my own ultrasound. Though it certainly is not the best medical decision to treat oneself, I felt justified because I would not have to bother my doctor during her holiday time or delay any longer. Fortunately, there was an open appointment time, and I got in the same day.

I shared my concern with the technologist doing the ultrasound, and she did additional views and called the radiologist, who reviewed them right away. She passed the phone to me, and he gave me the report as I was still lying beneath a cold sheet on the ultrasound table: "Eggshell calcifications with a cyst. Benign."

Great, I thought. No wait for the report, and all is well. Since "eggshell calcification" was new terminology for me as an emergency doctor, I did spend time looking things up on the Internet, and it seemed to make sense—a condition that occurs when fibrocystic breast disease ages. Yes, I would have to resign myself to the fact that the aging process was taking a toll on my body and move on with the plans for the spring.

In January 2008, the "cyst" was even larger, so I thought I should at least get it removed or drained. I did not want it to become a problem during my travels to China. I discussed it casually with a few female doctor buddies, and they agreed. I tried to make an appointment with the surgeon, but her office required a primary-doctor referral. After that, I attempted to schedule with my doctor, but the soonest that fit into my calendar was the end of February. I was reluctant to push for anything earlier as I knew from personal experience that doctors are busy, dealing daily with patients experiencing life-threatening diseases. There had already been a mammogram and two benign ultrasounds in the past six months, so surely a few extra days would not hurt anything.

Finally, the appointment time came. After I gave the doctor my factual update and requested a surgical referral for drainage of the cyst, she proceeded to the exam. The concerned look on her face exposed my secret fear. She paused and then shared her impression as calmly as she could. Her quavering voice reflected her concern. "I think…I think this might be cancer, and we need to do some further tests today."

Cancer? Instantly the tears gushed as my dam of denial was broken into pieces. Though her words were spoken gently, they felt like a death-sentence proclamation. In my mind, cancer was linked to death. My mind raced ahead, and I choked out the pain of my heart: "What will happen to my girls?"

It was a Friday afternoon, and I was the last patient of the day, but instead of that week winding down in her office, suddenly activity increased exponentially. I had an ECG to prepare me for surgery, blood was taken for lab work to determine my tumor markers (clues to cancer circulating in the bloodstream), and then there was a CAT scan of my chest and abdomen that afternoon. Based on the changes that had occurred in the less than nine months since my "normal" mammogram, she was certain we would see metastatic disease. Things were moving fast now. No more delays.

The technologist at the imaging department recognized me. It is hard to hide as a doctor in a small community of about forty thousand people. After the CAT scan, I spoke with the radiologist, a friend I had worked with for more than fifteen years. Together, we looked over the scan, and he reported his findings: "Benign."

That was a beautiful, comforting word, but still an unsettling feeling persisted. I told him I could feel and see the mass and insisted on more reassurance. Why is it not showing up on this latest and greatest digital imaging? He looked again. Nothing.

More physician opinions were needed. The following Monday, I was sandwiched into a lunch-hour slot with the first available surgeon. After his exam, he reported his gut feeling to me.

"Benign."

He did encourage me to proceed with the scheduled mammogram a few days later. The second one in eight months! For those who would like a better understanding of a woman's reluctance to undergo a mammogram, I suggest you stick a very sensitive part of your body into a hamburger press and compress as hard as you can. I am sure fibrocystic disease makes the exam more challenging, and the techs try to make the experience of a mammogram as reasonable as possible, but it remains uncomfortable at best. This time, with the increased size of the breast, it was downright painful. I resigned myself to the possibility it could be a novel therapeutic approach, popping the cyst and resolving all concerns. She repeated and repeated and repeated the process, attempting to get a digital image that would correlate to the changes that were visible. Usually, just a few images are taken, but this time, there were ten. Afterward, the radiologist was on the phone with me again.

"Normal. Benign." He continued, "I know the tech said there is obviously something there, but I can't see anything."

This time, I was unwilling to accept the diagnosis. I told him I could see it and feel it, and it was growing. Something was there—we should be able to see it on the CAT scan, mammogram, or ultrasound. He suggested we repeat the ultrasound even if it did not reveal anything the previous two times.

Lying on the ultrasound table for the third time in eight months, I hoped to find an answer, but I also still hoped it was not serious. The table was cold, but the words of the radiologist were even colder, like frozen icicles dangling above my chest, threatening to freeze my heart.

"There is a mass, and it has its own blood supply to it."

All I could picture was an alien living inside me. Obviously, I had watched too many horror movies in my earlier days.

He went on to explain I would need a biopsy with ultrasound guidance, but he did not perform that procedure. I needed to wait until that could be coordinated through my doctor's office and scheduled at a different facility. That meant patiently listening for another phone call. More delays. At least I had finally found someone who agreed there was a problem deep within me.

Through a series of unprecedented scheduling efforts, I was given an appointment that afternoon for the biopsy. I think the fact that I was a physician made the difference. Panic was spreading like wildfire among my comrades in medical practices in our small community. The new radiologist, being strategically guided by ultrasound, hit the undesired target, inserting the needle deep into the tissue, and collected multiple specimens. He reported he was fairly confident that it was cancer, but there were a few other types of benign problems that were still possible. His words gave me hope, but this was not reflected in his eyes. As I was leaving, the nurse assisting him gave me a book on breast cancer. Reality placed the last deep crack in my foundation of denial, and it shattered. I took the book home but did not open it for weeks—to do so was to begin a chapter I did not want to read or live. In the swirl of conflicting opinions, I still held out a microscopic sliver of hope. I waited for the pathologist's diagnosis, which would come after the analysis of the cells from deep within the mass. Would it be benign or cancerous?

The next day, in between taking care of patients in crisis in my emergency department, I called the pathologist to settle the score on my own personal crisis. It is not an odd thing for a physician to call a pathologist for a report, but it definitely is when the physician is the patient. There are some advantages to being a doctor, and I was tired of waiting in the traditional way that most of the world does. Yes, he responded, the analysis was complete, and the results were final. He hesitated briefly before proceeding. "Invasive pleomorphic lobular carcinoma." Denial died completely in that moment. I had breast cancer.

Cancer

It is one of the most powerful words in the world. It reroutes daily plans and ultimately changes everyone in its path. It has a far-reaching ripple effect on family, friends, and acquaintances. In the instant the pathological diagnosis was spoken, a great divide happened in my life: BC versus AC. Life before cancer and life after cancer. Nothing can desensitize someone to cancer. People have nicknamed it "the big *C*" just to avoid saying the word. Despite all the occasions I had helped various patients on their journeys with cancer, I was in no way prepared for my own. Yes, the thought had entered my mind on multiple occasions in the previous eight months, especially the last week, but until that final pathology report, I still held out some hope. Now I could not ignore the facts as shared by the American Cancer Society. Cancer is a common condition: More than a million people would be diagnosed with cancer in 2008, and forty thousand would die. Breast cancer alone affects one in eight women.[1]

Research dominated my free time. About 85–90 percent of breast cancers are ductal, meaning they form in the ducts or drainage tubes of the breasts. This is where milk travels on the way out the nipple. These cancers are easier to see on mammograms and tend to be found during exams as hard breast lumps. About 5 percent of breast cancer cases are a rare form of inflammatory breast cancer that initially looks like an infection but is, in fact, a very aggressive form of cancer. The final 5–10 percent are lobular cancers, which form in the lobes where milk is produced. This form is usually slower growing cells lining up in single file, making it very difficult, if not impossible, to see on a mammogram. It is especially difficult if a woman has dense breasts, as noted in my previous mammogram reports. Women with these findings are advised to have magnetic resonance imaging (MRI) to detect stealthy changes accurately. Unfortunately, this test costs about two thousand dollars, so insurance companies will not cover it unless there is a known significant family risk factor or a cancer diagnosis.

My biopsy results bought me a ticket to an MRI, which confirmed that the mass was deep, close to the chest wall, and spiculated, encompassing more than 7.5 centimeters (about three inches). This was much larger than anyone anticipated. I had noticed the thickening, but this was really just the tip of the iceberg. Later that day, a very concerned radiologist reading this MRI image called me at home to make sure I understood the seriousness of this result.

I did. I had a huge, ugly cancer, and I needed a huge, loving God with a huge miracle. This was not a small kidney stone that would quickly pass. The uncertainty was astounding. My brain would not turn off. The barrage of questions kept me awake at night:

How could this be happening to me? I lived such a healthy lifestyle.

Would I be treated locally or at the major cancer center three hours away?

What was my prognosis? How much more time did I have on earth?

Would I wither away in pain slowly and in agony or go quickly with very little warning?

Should I spend time cleaning the garage or with friends and loved ones?

What would happen to my teenage daughters yet to graduate from high school and college?

The *whys* began to swirl. Why, why, why? Why did I have to be diagnosed with an unusual cancer that could not be found earlier? Why now, just weeks before the departure of the team to China? Why so many delays and detours?

Best-selling author Dr. James Dobson, founder of Focus on the Family, an educational organization, spent more than twenty-four years as a marriage and family psychologist with many encounters with those in crisis asking, "Why did God let this happen to me?" He writes, "Here are the typical components of a 'Faith under Fire': a very troubling event, an element of injustice or unfairness, a silent God who could have intervened but didn't and a million unanswered questions. Have you ever been there?"[3]

Once again, I turned to the story of Lazarus in the Bible (John 11:1–45):

> Now a man named Lazarus was sick. He was from Bethany, the village of Mary and her sister Martha…So the sisters sent word to Jesus, "Lord, the one you love is sick." When He heard this, Jesus said, "This sickness will not end in death. No, it is for God's glory so that God's Son may be glorified through it." Jesus loved Martha and her sister and Lazarus. Yet when he heard that Lazarus was sick, He stayed where He was two more days…On His arrival, Jesus found that Lazarus had already been in the tomb for four days…"Lord," Martha said to Jesus, "if you had been here, my brother would not have died."

Jesus told his followers this was for God's glory, but the pain was still evident on their faces. The "if only you" was an overwhelming echo, and Jesus wept seeing the friends and family of Lazarus—his close friends—in such grief. Death appeared to be the victor once again; the hero lost, and the villain won. Only the most calloused soul likes such terrible endings. But Lazarus's story did not end with death. God had more plans for him. By God's grace, his story did not end in the grave; he was really at the beginning of a whole new chapter in his life.

> Jesus, once more deeply moved, came to the tomb…"Take away the stone," He said. "But Lord," said Martha…"by this time there is a bad odor, for he has been there four days."

> Then Jesus said, "Did I not tell you that if you believed, you would see the glory of God?"…Jesus called in a loud voice, "Lazarus, come out!" The dead man came out, his hands and feet wrapped with strips of linen, and a cloth around his face…Therefore, many of the Jews who

had come to visit Mary and had seen what Jesus did, put their faith in Him (NIV).

The call from the Great Physician went forth, and Lazarus left behind his grave clothes. His heart started beating again, and he breathed fresh air into his lungs. There is nothing impossible for God to overcome, not even death.

As I read the story, I wondered, “Will I hear that call as well and leave behind this cloak of death?” Like blindfolded, motionless Lazarus in the tomb, I waited helplessly for the grace of a God who sees all things and is working for my good and His glory.

Dear Lord,

I believe your timing is always perfect. May my perceived delays and detours result in your glory. Help my unbelief during this time of my faith under fire.

Amen.

Notes

1. American Cancer Society, https://www.cancer.org/.
2. http://www.graceclinicconline.org.
3. J. C. Dobson, *In the Arms of God* (Wheaton, IL: Tyndale House Publishers Inc., 1997). Part 3 pg1.

CHAPTER 4

Called to a New Purpose

And we know that in all things God works for the good of those who love Him, who have been called according to His purpose.

—Romans 8:28 (NIV)

As the delays gave way to a diagnosis, I had to quickly move away from denial and begin to strategize. What was my priority on my to-do list now? Instead of determining which patient was in the greatest life-threatening crisis or balancing the various needs of my daughters, I needed to focus on my health. My mind went into overdrive, planning as best as I could with limited information. My boss had to be informed, my work shifts had to be dispersed among my partners, oncologist visited, surgeon consulted, and placement of a port (an implantable device to allow for easy venous access for chemotherapy) scheduled. I had to alert the team going to China that I would not be able to join them and assign team members to take on my leadership responsibilities. Those were the easy, intellectual tasks.

The most challenging task for me was the emotionally charged news I would need to share with my family. The *C* word was not an unknown entity to my birth family. In my late twenties, the day before my medical school interview, my father was diagnosed with metastatic colon cancer. Over the subsequent six months, we watched a once very strong and opinionated New Yorker turn into a depressed, despondent, tearful, and desperately confused patient. In 1987 he was given chemo, but really, there was no hope for his survival. He died a few months into my first semester of medical school, right in the midst of those mind-swirling days of anatomy, microbiology, biochemistry, and sleep deprivation. Medical school would allow only so many days of absence before you were dropped. Many sacrifices had to be made throughout medical school, and we all lost time with our families. My father loved to be out on the open seas with the wind in his face sailing his twenty-one-foot boat. I wished I had more sailing days with him.

Death had already made a second visit to our family. During a warm August day in 2005, my only brother, Fred, was hiking alone north of Yosemite, California. This was a treacherous but beautiful area, filled with mountain peaks and the aroma of evergreens. Fred was a seasoned hiker, loved high adventure on the road less traveled, and enjoyed memorializing the beauty that God had created. He would capture the sights and sounds around him on film and audiotape, sharing them with friends and family. Some of his best photos would beckon him to go where no man had gone before with the reward of a prized ribbon in one of the various visual art competitions around San Francisco. His final steps were too close to the edge of eternity.

In his last phone call, he left birthday greetings for me on the answering machine. We were always very close, with only one year separating us in chronological age. He shared his favorite band with me and dedicated songs to me during lunch at high school. I made him a quilted shirt with a full spectrum of colors so he could fit in with the popular style of the '70s. We often hiked and camped with our children at sites around California.

He never returned from that hike, and his presumed death brought frequent tsunami-size waves of grief to our family. My dear mother was hit especially hard during the holidays with the sadness, but we all grappled with bringing closure on such a tragic and unexpected event. How does a parent ever find closure after the loss of a child, even if he was forty-six years old? How could I give my mother any hope that she would not be saying a final good-bye to yet another of her grown children in her forties?

However, even more difficult than sharing the news with my mother and two sisters would be divulging the secret to my greatest treasures, my two teenage daughters. At this point they knew nothing of my journey on this bumpy and uncertain road of tests, biopsies, and imaging exams. Why cause fear and alarm since I had been reassured all along that my lump was benign? Even as the pathology reports and imaging results brought some undeniable data, I was still hesitant to share my burden with them. I had supported them through the years of their highs and lows. I had been the stabilizing foundation in our home. Now I was living with shaky uncertainty how my next week would play out, let alone beyond.

I decided it would have to be done face-to-face during the following week. My elder daughter was returning from college for spring break, and we would have more time together. Though the time could be set, the reactions were harder to predict. What I did know was that they would react differently from each other. Though they had developed from the same genetic pool, some would say my girls were as different as day and night. The fact that they were born on extreme ends of the clock, one at about 12:30 p.m. and one at 12:30 a.m., may support that belief. I do know that, despite the various arguments on nature and nurture, these girls came into this world with very different likes, dislikes, and personalities. The elder one was quiet and loved her alone time, rainy days, and cats, not necessarily in that order. She was very disciplined and studious, rising early to begin her day.

The younger one, on the other hand, loved to sleep in as a teenager (don't call before 10:00 a.m.!), absorbed the sun like a sponge any chance she could, and was particularly fond of staying up late talking to friends. And of course, just to be different, she loved dogs and wasn't fond of studying.

Together, we loved to travel to many places on family outings and mission trips. We worked as a team to pray for others, memorize scriptures, and conquer the household responsibilities. We had a special language all of our own when it came to playing charades with the extended family, and we usually were overwhelmingly victorious. I was so proud of my girls and balanced the nurturing cheerleader role with the role of the mama bear should anyone try to hurt them. We were the Snyder girls.

In 2008 they were in different chapters of their own life stories. The older one was well into her first year of college at the University of Idaho as a math major...far enough away to live away from home but close enough for a weekend visit with us, a quick return home to Mom's cooking or a mystery party with friends. The younger one was chronologically fourteen years old but liked living like she was twenty-one. She had already traveled to many countries with me as I provided medical care and training in Kenya, Brazil, Venezuela, Turkey, and China. She was a fledgling eaglet wanting to soar, but instead, she found herself grounded due to some judgment and navigational errors. We regularly had verbal boxing matches in which she would fine-tune her debate skills and leave her mother stammering, "Because I said so." I had no idea how she would take the unwelcome news.

My plan was to say it very matter-of-factly during weekly catch-up time—perhaps something like this: "Grandma will visit next week, household chores need to be finished, and I'll need a ride to the hospital Wednesday to get my chemo port placed for cancer treatment." Though well calculated and planned, the emotionally detached version did not happen that day. As I looked into their eyes, the words "I have cancer" escaped, took my breath away, and left me grabbing for facial tissues. The emotional dam broke once more, and the tears gushed forth uncontrollably.

I will never know all the thoughts that flashed through their minds during that moment. I wanted to be strong and encouraging and tell them with all certainty that I would be there for their high-school and college graduations years away, their weddings, and even beyond to the birth of their first children—but that was not possible. I did not honestly know if I would spend Christmas again this side of heaven. I wanted to tell them that life would continue on, as if this was just something else on my to-do list, but I knew that would not be the truth. I did not know or feel that everything was going to work out OK. Life itself had become uncertain, and I was having a hard time keeping my own footing in this storm, let alone being able to support them as the waves came crashing down.

I told them what I could, struggling to articulate my words between blowing my nose and dabbing my eyes. I would start chemo the week after the port was placed. I would lose my hair in about three weeks. I would wear a wig, so I wouldn't embarrass them around their friends. My typically high energy would be affected, but I was not sure how much. Unable to debate this life-changing moment, the younger one dashed to her room, escaping from the torrent of emotion.

As I sat quietly with tearstains growing on my dress, I felt the loving arms and words of my elder daughter: "It will be OK, Mom. It will all work out."

In that instant, the timeless words of Romans 8:28 disarmed my fear: "And we know that in all things God works for the good of those who love Him, who have been called according to His purpose" (NIV).

In my brokenness, my firstborn child was a source of strength, reminding me of that eternal truth.

Truth. What is truth? All humanity desires it, looking left and right for glimpses. It's a question asked by philosophers and theologians worldwide throughout time. Even scientists are in their own search for truth, trying to develop their knowledge base through the scientific method of analysis. Politicians notoriously struggle with telling their supporters the whole truth. A few memorable quotes about truth:

> A lie can travel halfway around the world while
> the truth is putting on its shoes.
>
> —Mark Twain

> Rather than love, than money, than fame, give me truth.
>
> —Henry David Thoreau

> Better a cruel truth than a comfortable delusion.
>
> —Edward Abbey

> So, Jesus said to the Jews who believed him, "If you abide
> in my word, you are truly my disciples, and you will
> know the truth, and the truth will set you free."
>
> —John 8:31–32

When Jesus was on trial, he said, "For this purpose I was born and for this purpose I have come into the world-to bear witness to the truth. Everyone who is of the truth listens to my voice" (John 18:37, ESV).

The truth is that I was terminal from the day I was born. All of us are terminal. We breathe a first breath and a last. Regardless of the normal life expectancy, no one is guaranteed to live to five or seventy-five years of age. There is no expiration date embossed on our belly buttons. No one really knows when his or her time will come. Humans were designed to live eternally, but not in these decaying, disease- and pain-riddled bodies. Adam and Eve, the parents of all humankind, chose to disobey the plan God gave them for living their lives in a beautiful garden, and all generations after them had to pay the price. The arsenic of living in a fallen world has permeated the human race and our universe.

Decades working in the ED and experiencing life left me with indelible memories of emotional pain as people longed for more time. It was seen in the tear-filled faces of the parents of a stillborn baby, the eyes of the young girl desperately holding the lifeless body of her brother, the whisper of the newlywed standing beside the twisted vehicle of his lover, and the heartfelt sob of the ninety-year-old woman at her husband's bedside as his heart stopped.

Destined for eternity but proportionally, only a millisecond of time was designed to be spent in this world. Just as the eyes developed in a baby's head in the darkness of the womb prepare the child for the world of sight outside the womb, we, too, are being prepared for a world beyond this one. It is there we will live as we have been designed, eternally free from the pain of this world. This earthly world is merely preparation, contrasting sharply with the sweetness of the heavenly, eternal life ahead—where there will be no more good-byes, sorrow, or suffering.

So what were God's purpose and plan for the remainder of my numbered days on earth?

The next verse, Romans 8:29, held the answer: "For those God foreknew He also predestined to be conformed to the likeness of His Son, that He might be the firstborn among many brothers" (NIV).

The "all things working out for the good" meant I would, somehow, through the good, bad, and ugly parts of the journey, be conformed to His likeness. Somehow receiving weekly cell-killing chemotherapy instead of giving life-saving treatments to others would be used by God to shape and mold me to reflect Him better in the hurting world around me. Life on planet earth does not always make sense with our limited knowledge base but can be appreciated visually in tapestry work. The woven threads of dark colors cause the lighter sections to stand out and become more defined. Together, they balance and bring the beautiful masterpiece into clear focus. I must accept all the threads that are a part of his handiwork in me, whether they seem to be dark or light. They all have value. My new purpose would be found when I fully surrendered to his master design.

He is the producer, director, and potter. His hands will mold me as a potter with soft clay and, in the process, remove some parts and add other components so I can be useful for His purposes.

"Then the word of the Lord came to me…Like clay in the hand of the potter, so are you in My hand" (Jer. 18:5–6, NIV).

Dear Lord,

Mold me as a piece of clay and help me to remain soft and pliable in Your nail-scarred hands. You know the pain we feel because You chose to leave the splendors of a pain-free heaven to come to earth and take on our pain and sin so we can live eternally with You without any more pain, tears, or sorrow. There You will forever wipe away all tears for You have been victorious over death. I do trust that You will somehow work all things out for the good and conform me to the likeness of Your Son for Your glory.

Amen.

CHAPTER 5

Comfort and Compassion

Too often we underestimate the power of a touch, a smile, a kind word, a listening ear, an honest compliment, or the smallest act of caring, all of which have the potential to turn a life around.

—Leo Buscaglia

Life dangled treacherously, as if by a fraying string, for Jessica McClure on October 14, 1987. The world sat mesmerized, eyes fixed to their televisions, as the real-life, real-time drama of this precious eighteen-month-old child unfolded before their eyes. That bright morning, she was out for a walk in her neighborhood, exploring the world around her. But her walk abruptly ended when she fell into a dry well, twenty-two feet below the ground. There she would remain in darkness, wounded with a broken arm and hopeless without the help of a hero.

She was in Midland, Texas, but it felt like this could have been in my own backyard. All corners of the globe were watching and waiting…she was in our lives and in our hearts. Prayers ascended, rescue workers converged, and brainstorming came from all corners of the globe. Various methods of extrication were attempted around the clock for fifty-seven hours—all to no avail. We all sensed time was ticking on, and we did not know if she could hold on. At one point, I did not know if I wanted to continue to watch the news and become more and more emotionally invested in the life of a stranger. It would be so painful if she died. But I was helplessly pulled in by an invisible magnet of compassion. I was drawn to her and unable to disengage. I lived hundreds of miles away, but my heart was with her and her family.

In that final hour of waiting, water became her hope. A water jet cutter is a tool capable of slicing into metal or other materials using a jet of water at high velocity and pressure. Water at the right pressure, at the right location, and at the right time was the hope to free Jessica. It reminded me of the intervention when a duck becomes stuck in a dry well. Gently adding water will allow the duck to rise, spread its wings, and to free itself from its tomb.

As Jessica broke out of darkness into light on October 16, 1987, people from around the world celebrated. Her victory was our victory. Years later, on May 30, 2007, *USA Today* ranked McClure twenty-second on its list of "Twenty-Five Lives of Indelible Impact." I know she had an impact on mine with her tenacity.

Jessica had a fairy-tale ending, though she did not go unscathed and required a toe amputation and fifteen different surgeries over the past twenty-five years as a result of her ordeal. She married and was blessed with two children of her own to comfort in their fearful days. Unfortunately, things did not end as well for her hero.

Author D. Lance Lunsford wrote *The Rainbow's Shadow: The True Stories of the Baby Jessica Rescue and the Tragedies That Followed*, which was published in 2005.[1] In this book, he reports that paramedic Robert O'Donnell was instrumental in Jessica's rescue and held her closely in his arms as she was lifted to safety but unfortunately suffered from posttraumatic stress disorder after the intense rescue efforts. In 1995 he succumbed to his despair and killed himself.

WOULD A GREATER DOSE OF COMFORT AT THE RIGHT TIME HAVE SAVED HIS LIFE IN HIS DESPERATE HOUR?

Suicide is a very significant cause of death. According to the Centers for Disease Control and Prevention (CDC), in 2015: [2]

- Suicide was the tenth leading cause of death overall in the United States, claiming the lives of more than 44,000 people.

- Suicide was the third leading cause of death among individuals between the ages of 10 and 14, and the second leading cause of death among individuals between the ages of 15 and 34.
- There were more than twice as many suicides (44,193) in the United States as there were homicides (17,793).

As an ED physician, I would see an increase in suicide attempts during the holidays, and one particular night, there were five patients who had attempted suicide. How do we restore hope to the hopeless and provide transformative comfort to those in need?

What does comfort look like, smell like, or feel like to you? When was it most needed in your life?

Maybe it is that irresistible smell of hot homemade bread or the aroma of a light-brown Thanksgiving turkey roasting in the oven, with apple and pumpkin pies on the counter. As you walk through the door into Mom's house, you know you are home. Maybe it is crawling into your cozy recliner beside the brightly lit fireplace on a rainy day, warming your hands with a mug of steamy hot chocolate. The descriptions are endless and as personal as fingerprints. Ultimately, comfort is the sense of safety, love and, hope all bundled into one moment. The sweetness of the comfort intensifies with the magnitude of the despair.

I cannot relate to the amazing rescue that Jessica experienced or to the desperation that Robert, her rescuer, must have felt in his darkest hour. However, I can relate to the duck hopelessly stuck in darkness, needing to be brought into the light, to fly again. April 1, 2008, was more than just another April Fools' Day and will live in infamy in my journal of life. In the United States on April 1, people often scheme to play a practical joke on someone they know, and some go to extremes to convince the other person of the new "reality" and to cause the person to feel foolish when the truth is revealed. It is all done in jest, and the joke is usually short lived.

That particular morning, I was about three weeks into living out the cancer diagnosis and more than two weeks into treatment. Though the fatigue from the poison of chemo flowing through my veins pinned me like a chain to my bed, I was determined to meet with my Partners for Life team at the airport. I donned a soft pink cap to cover the thinning shreds of hair and to broadcast my personal strength at the moment. I knew I had to give them my send-off good-bye and prayers as they headed for China, many of them taking the more-than-fifteen-hour flight for the first time. I reminded them that though I could not lead them on their trip, God would continue to guide and direct them.

Right up to their departure day, I tried to bargain with my oncologist to let me go with them. They could carry my suitcases. I could return early if I got worse. What if I took a break from weekly chemo for just a few weeks? Consistently the answer was an adamant no. As I drove home from the airport alone, the tears gushed forth once again and soaked my clothing. All hope of going with the team as planned was dashed into a million pieces and scattered into the wind.

Proverbs 3:12 reminds us, "Hope deferred makes the heart sick, but a dream fulfilled is a tree of life" (NLT). In the busyness of preparing the team, maintaining home life, working the occasional emergency department shift, and starting chemo, I had not grieved—not grieved the loss of my health and any sense of control I thought I had.

Emotionally and hormonally, I was a wreck. Because the cancer was "estrogen-receptor positive," all estrogen hormonal supplementation had been suddenly cut off, and I was in withdrawal. It hit me like a ton of bricks. My fatigue and hot flashes increased; memory decreased. My hair had been falling out on my pillow for the past week, and I had a few wigs staring at me from the corner of my room, ready to wear. The reality of my weakness and desperate state sank into my very core. Like a solo jungle explorer who stumbles into quicksand, I was sinking in the mire of hopelessness and felt incredibly alone.

After arriving home from the airport, I cut off the dangling remains of thirteen inches of hair and placed the pink stretch cap quickly back on to hide my naked skull. Baldness was expected and initially seemed a small price to pay to stop the growth of the aggressively advancing tumor. Now we had reached our stalemate. Daily examinations revealed there was no shrinkage of the tumor.

The "why" and "when" questions stealthily crept in to attack and pierce my very heart of faith. Why were these drugs not killing the tumor? When was the miraculous Lazarus-type healing going to happen?

I believed and prayed it would come and still no healing.

Others believed, and I was on prayer chains around the world and still no healing.

I rested, reduced my doctor work to one day a week, followed all my doctor's instructions, tried cancer remedies like mushroom extract and tofu, and was an overall compliant patient and still no healing.

I sat alone and wept in the bright light of my garden oasis. I was surrounded by the beauty of God's amazing creative nature, His gift to me, yet I was blinded by the tears of a dark hopelessness. I called out to God to help me during this time of being in the dark spiritual well.

Suddenly and unexpectedly, I received a call from my friend Shelley. Somehow, she knew when I responded that I was OK that I really was not. She dropped her plans for the rest of the morning, left her important work behind, and came and sat with me, listening to my grief and losses. Her presence was powerful. This was not the first time she had walked the cancer journey with someone. Not too long before that day, she had walked it with her mother. That lost battle was still fresh in her heart. Through that season she had experienced a comfort that would later allow her to overflow with comfort for others. It was through her pain that she developed more compassion for those who suffered like her mother did. It was through her pain that she understood mine. Together that day, we rode the full spectrum of colorful emotions: we cried, laughed, and prayed for the strength I would need. The water trickled down the edge of the well, and this duck began to see light and spread her wings. Hope was restored. My heart was mended, and I knew I would fly again.

"Praise be to the God and Father of our Lord Jesus Christ, the Father of compassion and the God of all comfort who comforts us in all our troubles, so that we can comfort those in any trouble with the comfort we ourselves have received from God" (2 Cor. 1:3, NIV).

Comfort is packaged in humanity. As I became better at expressing my needs, others brought their personal gifts and talents to help buoy me up. Through cards, e-mails, acts of kindness, and listening ears, they provided the strength I would need for the battle to come.

We all need the infilling of God's love through the comforting hands of His people. Those who experienced the comfort of the Lord in their various life circumstances knew best how to come alongside me in my time of need and were true funnels, assisting with the infusion of His love.

Lord, thank You for being the God of all comfort and compassion, who knows when we need Your touch expressed with human touch. Thank You that You know how to get the stuck ducks out of wells, in Your way and in Your time, so we can comfort others!
Amen.

Notes

1. D. Lance Lunsford, *The Rainbow's Shadow: The True Stories of the Baby Jessica Rescue and the Tragedies That Followed* (Haywood, CA: Bristol Publishing Enterprises, 2005).
2. https://www.nimh.nih.gov/health/statistics/suicide.shtml.

CHAPTER 6

Living in the Shadow of Death

The Lord is my shepherd, I shall not be in want. He makes me lie down in green pastures, He leads me beside quiet waters, He restores my soul. He guides me in paths of righteousness for His name's sake. Even though I walk through the valley of the shadow of death, I will fear no evil, for you are with me; your rod and your staff they comfort me.

—Psalm 23:1–4, NIV

Death. The word makes our skin crawl. Our minds envision terror, excruciating pain, dark cemeteries, and sun-scorched skeletons. Death is universal and no respecter of persons. Those with a birth date on this planet can expect to come to an end. Comfort in those final days is frequently found through the reading of this psalm found in the middle of the Bible. This collection of inspired writings with more than 3.9 billion copies in print is clearly the most translated and read book in the world. The next most read book is *Quotations from Chairman Mao Tse-Tung* at 8.2 million copies.[1] The Bible is divided into the Old Testament and the New Testament. The Old Testament contains the writings supported by the three major religions: Judaism, Christianity, and Islam. The New Testament records the actions and words of Jesus Christ and some of his followers. The sixty-six books contained in the Bible were written by thirty-five authors and span sixteen centuries. Amazingly, there is a consistent master theme of God's redemption in each of the writings.

In this passage from the Bible, the author reminds us that life is a journey and that the Lord will be shepherding us through our most difficult paths. Shepherds are uncommon in our high-tech electronic cities but very common in the green rural landscapes of most of the world. They can be young or old, in Israel, Mexico, or Africa, but all good shepherds share the same purpose: to preserve the safety and health of their sheep.

W. Phillip Keller is an author and a shepherd. In his book *A Shepherd Looks at Psalm 23*, he describes how the wise shepherd must take the sheep to various grazing lands to be safe from predators and to obtain adequate, well-balanced nutrition. A good shepherd will even put his or her own life at risk in defending the sheep from a ravenous wolf. At times, the sheep will be resting at home in their pen, but then they are moved quickly by the shepherd for their own good, regardless of whether or not they understand why. Leaving our comfort zone for the haze of uncertainty brings a surge of fear to most, whether we are a wooly sheep or a human being.

Traveling requires flexibility. The familiar is exchanged for exposure to a new culture, new systems of communication, and adjustment to very unusual food choices. My traveling palate met up with the challenges of African black dried caterpillars, fermented horse milk in Mongolia, squirrel soup in Mexico, and chicken feet at a fine restaurant in China. Is it possible to feel at home while traveling? The saying "Home is where the heart is" reminds us that our home can be located anywhere. Houses come in many sizes and shapes, but as long as they are filled with those we love, they are home. The owners of forty-foot recreational vehicles understand this as they cart around family members and a good percentage of their earthly goods on various adventures. Though out of their comfort zones, they are surrounded by loving people, the heart of the home.

"What is your home like?"

The word "home" conjures up a vast array of pictures in my mind—walls made from the flattened, discarded cardboard boxes that I saw at the Tijuana garbage dump and a highly contrasting fairy-tale castle in the snowcapped Austrian Alps. During my sojourn of less than sixty years on earth, I have already laid my head to rest in more than three hundred different homes and lodgings. Some stays were only for a night, others for years, some were in the United States, and others in one of more than forty different countries. Needless to say, I strongly encourage all acquaintances to use pencil instead of pen when filling in my home address in their books. They need the option to erase! I have all the symptoms of incurable wanderlust, the endless urge to explore and seek greener pastures. I think there are a few reasons I learned to love traveling.

My first relocation was when I was three years old. My family decided to move from the cold, snowy winters of Detroit, Michigan, to the warm beach setting of San Diego, California. Though obviously too young to have a good recall of the transition, I am thankful for that decision. I have never developed an affinity for cold temperatures, and undoubtedly, it seems like a "greener pastures" type of move from my adult perspective.

Besides a quick visit to Tijuana, Mexico, as a teenager and a few camping trips and cross-country family vacations, during most of my days growing up, I was settled in one home with two parents and three siblings. My siblings have traveled as well, but none to the extent or with the frequency that I have. What I do know is that, for whatever reason, I was designed with an insatiable curiosity about new cultural experiences, and I thrive on the diversity of people.

My first real adventure away from home and my family was with the John F. Kennedy marching band as a high-school student in La Palma, California. We were invited to march in the Saint Patrick's parade in Dublin, Ireland, and we did everything possible to raise funds for the journey, from candy bar sales to car washes. As this group of Southern California teenagers left their parents half a world away and gazed upon the green, rolling hills of Ireland, we were like freshly weaned lambs frolicking in greener pastures. The urge to explore more of the world continued to grow in me.

My wanderings have taken me to many places, domestic and exotic, safe and dangerous, with unforgettable memories. Looking back, these memories would become faith builders to help me on my difficult life journey. On July 30, 1982, I was in search of a campground after deplaning in one of the northernmost cities in the United States—Point Barrow, Alaska. I had a well-stocked backpack, complete with a tent, food, a stove, and all the other necessary amenities. I asked the woman at the information desk where the closest campground was, and she looked at me as if I was speaking a foreign language. She told me there was no campground, but there was a hotel for two hundred dollars a night down the road. Because the planes only came in and left every two days, that was not going to work on my budget.

I decided to wander down the road and find an open area of tundra to set up my blue tarp and tent. I was ready for this new temporary home as I stood amazed watching the icebergs floating on the aqua-colored Arctic Sea. Though I felt chilled on this summer day, it was actually one of their warmest days on record, and the wolverine-parka-clad children were overheating. I was looking forward to being in a place that was light all through the night and stayed up late reading inside my tent.

At 2:00 a.m., with the sky still lit by the muted light of the sun, my sleep was disturbed by the sound of gunshots and the whiz of bullets passing over my tent. Obviously, I had found myself on unwelcoming soil. This wasn't a campground but rather Inuit Native American territory where I had mistakenly set down stakes. Male voices called out for me to come out of the tent. I felt my heart pound and called out to God. My only direction was to lie still and speechless but in continual prayer. I knew that if I died on my birthday, it would be very upsetting to my mother. As the footsteps approached, I heard the voices circling my tent and then the sound of the tent zipper opening...

This side of heaven, I won't know what stopped those men from entering my tent, but I speculate God had something to do with it. I lay still for about an hour and then gathered up my wet tent and belongings and proceeded to a church where I was welcomed in, and I could dry my tent. A church member provided an apartment accommodation for me for that second night in Point Barrow until my plane departed. This faith-building experience was merely an appetizer for what was to come.

After many years of wanting to experience life in Africa, an opportunity finally came in 1985 for me to use my nursing skills. I joined a group whose members were committed to bringing measles immunizations to Uganda, where so many children were dying from the epidemic. Unfortunately, our plans were rerouted when our plane became the last to land in Kampala at the commencement of the military coup and takeover of the government. My first clue that something was wrong was the lack of customs agents. When we descended from that airplane, we descended into chaos. People were running in every direction. Locals wielding guns fired them aimlessly into the air. By God's grace, we were rushed into a van that took us to a Christian conference center, where we were fed delicious meals with peanut sauce and were protected from attacks of red ants by the courageous staff. The women even danced for us in their traditional multicolored dresses and attempted to teach the American girls some African rhythm. They provided great distraction in between our sessions of listening to the BBC news updates regarding the status of the government. Fortunately, five days later, the US embassy representative arrived in a jeep with a red, white, and blue flag waving in the breeze. He relocated us to the British guesthouse where we could coordinate transportation through car caravans with the World Bank and the German embassy, whose personnel were also attempting to safely depart the country.

In contrast to that scary, chaotic arrival scene in Uganda, there were two times in Kenya, Africa, when goatskin-clad women welcomed us with their quiet and beautiful smiles. The first involved meeting with the blood-and-milk-painted Pokot tribal people, who greeted our group with the song "Give Me that Old Time Religion," accompanied by their ethnic drums. Later in 2004, my daughter and I visited the Samburu tribe in Kenya. We rode on light-brown smelly, grunting camels while our guide walked beside us on the dusty desert road leading to their small village. After proudly showing us their crafts, sparse huts, and how to start a fire using donkey dung as lighter fluid, they asked us to join them in their traditional "neck" dancing ritual. This was performed by only women and involved a lot of gyrations with the neck. My attempts resembled a teenage turtle. I am sure the laughter that overflowed that day will spill out of memories on two continents for many days to come! *Mzungu* (white people) trying to dance like native Africans was entertaining to all.

Christmas Day that year was tastefully memorable. My daughter and I were deep into the variegated green Amazon rainforest of Brazil, visiting our missionary friend Gilli. She was an amazing woman providing her nursing services, the only American in this community of more than twenty thousand people. During the short three-week visit, we attempted to provide what assistance we could when not distracted by tarantulas, a variety of spider the size of dinner plates, and armies of bloodsucking mosquitoes. I wondered what would be on the dinner menu. Thankfully, we enjoyed freshly caught piranha for dinner, and I saved the jaws and teeth as a souvenir, grateful that I found my teeth in its flesh rather than the other way around. The meal was accompanied by an unexpected but savory plate of spaghetti, served up as we sat on a Twister game mat. Yes, there was familiarity in the midst of our cultural differences! That would not be the last time that cultural practices took me by surprise.

In China, during our initial training visit in 2007, I found myself completely unprepared for the differences in expectations of a fire drill. The hospital administration had requested that our training team, which included a fire captain, assist them with preparing their hospital staff in the event of a fire. Drills are quite commonplace in US hospitals so they can maintain their accreditation, but they were a new adventure for our colleagues in Shanghai. During training, we typically use cardboard signs signifying fire in the hospital area being evaluated. After days of training the Chinese medical and hospital staff, we were informed that they were ready, and we commenced the drill. Our team was totally unprepared for finding an actual fire in a metal bin in the administrator's office! The interpreter told us that this was to add some dramatic realism for the five news reporters' cameras that had showed up to publicize the training event. The smoke and flames were more than the fire captain who had trained them was prepared for. The entire time we coughed and were worried that the whole hospital would go up in smoke. Finally, though, the film crew finished, and the fire was extinguished. Cultural preferences!

Life is full of surprises. Just when we think we have everything planned and under control, there is that unexpected life event completely changing our direction. In that spring of 2008, as the Partners for Life team went off on another adventure to China, I passed my time at the local community cancer center, my new home away from home. It was a bit like joining a new culture with its own language, schedules, and expected behaviors: the cancer community.

Weekly Taxol chemotherapy treatments and coordinated oncology visits, lab tests, and so on set the rhythm for my new pasture. The receptionist, office staff, and nurses became the new friends. I was deeply grateful I had medical insurance as I started on this very expensive road trip, frequently still thinking of those less fortunate medically uninsured patients at Grace Clinic. The oncology waiting room was more like a family room filled with other patients and their families. We talked, encouraged one another, or worked on puzzles while we waited for treatments. Though it was still difficult to believe that I belonged here, I had come to accept that this was a part of the trail that the Good Shepherd had directed me to walk. Sometimes the conversations with other patients would meander to their end-of-life fears and concerns. At times, I was able to pray with another traveler walking through this valley of the shadow of death.

Prayer with these other patients was an unexpected privilege that came as a gift with my diagnosis. It was a way to comfort others with the comfort I had already experienced from the Lord through the compassionate prayers of family and friends in their homes all over the world. Based on my medical training, I knew for some it would take more than modern medicine had to offer. A God-size miracle was needed to make it out of the valley alive, and any eternal direction I could offer would be appreciated. I viewed every chemo session as another divine opportunity to meet someone. I encountered young and old, rich and poor, all with a variety of wild traveling stories. We all shared the common thread of cancer, striving to survive.

This new culture contrasted sharply with my previous time-efficient, productivity-focused lifestyle. Sleeping, naps, and waiting dominated this culture. Rest came to me as I experienced the reality of "He makes me to lie down in green pastures." I am not accustomed to sitting down for long, and the emergency department shifts would frequently keep me on my feet fairly continuously for twelve to fourteen hours a day. By nature, I rarely would relax and watch a movie without multitasking. With this new pasture, lying down and taking naps was a radical but necessary change in my lifestyle. Every day, as a result of the chemo, there was increasing fatigue as billions of cells, both good and bad, were being killed. My body was in overdrive to restore new healthy cells. Also, following the chemo infusions, I was sedated with a dose of medications that would prevent potential allergic reactions to the chemo drug, which left me nonfunctional for hours. I was forced to lie down and rest.

Laughter had to be sprinkled into the day to keep my sanity. I smiled as I imagined that the "quiet waters" were the pink intravenous solutions that would subsequently exit my body in an orange hue—certainly an unexpected turn of events! Wig jokes and old comedy movies helped. The Lord's "rod of correction" came to me as I spent additional time each day reading the Bible and other Christian books. He taught me to be still before Him. It was a particularly helpful season to reassess unresolved issues of forgiveness and to "restore my soul." I was reminded how much He wants us to walk in complete healing. As prayer warriors continued to ask God for a complete healing, I felt the peace that passes all understanding wash over me, allowing me truly to rest without anxiety or grudges.

Without the intense work schedule I had in the past, I now had time to do some research in the field of oncology. For most of the common cancers, a major cause has been identified: smoking causes 90 percent of lung cancer worldwide, hepatitis virus causes most primary liver cancers, *Helicobacter pylori* bacteria causes many of the stomach cancers, and the human papillomavirus causes cervical cancer. Colon cancer is largely explained by a combination of lack of physical activity, low-fiber diet, and family history. Breast cancer increases with the use of supplemental hormones, whether as a birth control pill before menopause or estrogen afterward. Genetics are known risk factors. Additionally, cancer risk can depend on where you are born and raised. Women in North America and Northern Europe have five times the risk of women in Asia and Africa. A study on Japanese immigrants to California showed first-generation women had the same risk of breast cancer as their parents in Japan, but the second and third generations demonstrated the same risk as Caucasian American women.[2] Through research in epigenetics, we now know that both minimizing exposures to toxins and maximizing proper nutrition have the power to turn off our genes and to influence disease manifestation. We do not have to completely expect genetic diseases to manifest, but we have some ability to alter our health trajectory.

During this time of personal research, a friend of mine shared a medical journal with me that opened up more questions about vitamins and cancer.

Vitamin D specifically affects the risk of metastasis and the functioning of the immune system, so I ordered my own test. When I learned of my significant deficit (my level was unmeasurable—less than seven nanograms per milliliter on a normal scale of thirty to one hundred nanograms per milliliter), I researched further what this meant. At that time, the oncologist I was seeing had not heard of the impact of subtherapeutic vitamin-D levels. This factor alone increased my risk for metastatic disease because normal levels are needed to allow the T lymphocytes to turn into macrophages (like little Pac-men) to gobble up invaders and abnormal cells. This vital role of vitamin D was not known when I went to medical school years before. We were taught its primary role had to do with strengthening bones and preventing rickets (bow legs). Milk, fortified dairy products, oily fish, and sunlight were common sources of this vitamin. By 2010, the medical and lay literature were packed with studies and information on the broad impact therapeutic levels of vitamin D could have. Obviously, despite living in the desert, I needed supplementation.[3]

This was the season that the Good Shepherd "led me into all righteousness," revealing the answer to many mysteries. The low vitamin D level explained all the strange symptoms that I had been experiencing for years: the muscle weakness, hair loss, and osteopenia (thin bones). I shared this newfound information with friends and family, and many found they had low levels of vitamin D and needed prescription dosages for correction. I was grateful for this time of "pasture" that gave me the time to understand something that could help preserve the health of my friends and family. Even though I was in a difficult season of bad health, I knew that God was with me. I need not fear evil.

The most frequent question I heard during this valley time was, "How are you doing?" During the worst days, I had a choice to walk in the shadow of death or to walk in the newness of life. The shadow of death is just an illusion of what might fully happen. Just an idea: people read the Twenty-third Psalm all the time, seeing it as a comforting passage for dark times. However, now I understood it in another way. The specter of death loomed over me every day as I wondered how many days I had left. It was if I was a sheep walking through a cavern, and the shadow of a wolf appeared—but only the shadow ever drew near. I was not alone. The Shepherd was with me. I did not face the wolf alone.

Was I ready to die? At the age of fifteen in a small church in California, I had accepted Jesus's death on the cross as payment for my sins, and at that moment, my life and eternal destiny changed. The fear of eternity spent in hell, where there would be endless pain and suffering, was gone. I had peace that no matter how long my life was on earth death would not have any sting or power over me. I had been promised eternal life with Jesus. Nothing would separate me from Him or His love. This gave me incredible courage most days.

However, there were those occasional days when the weight of cancer diagnosis and potential separation from my family and friends weighed on me. Fear would creep in, and hopelessness would begin to reign. Tears would fall once again, and I would feel I was unraveling at the seams.

During one of those particularly difficult days, I came upon an e-mail by evangelist Louie Giglio, describing a discovery about human cellular biology. With the advent of the electron microscope, so many interdependent functions of our bodies have been revealed. He described the "glue" that keeps our cells all together, which scientists call the glycoprotein laminin. It can be seen under the electron microscope, and its structure is depicted below:[4]

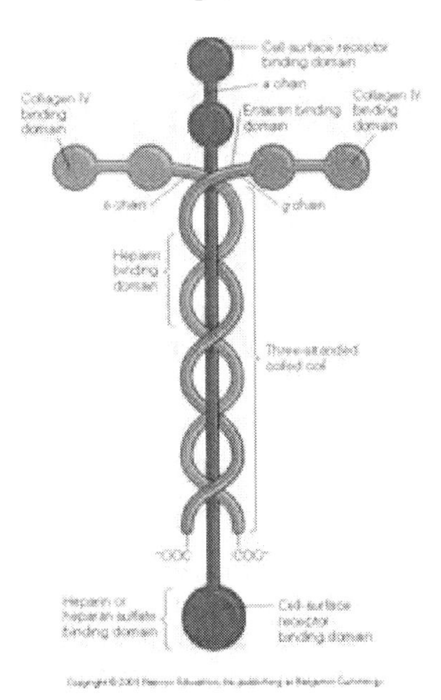

What holds our cells together and keeps us from falling apart is a protein shaped like a cross, the eternal reminder of the sacrificial love of Jesus Christ.

> He is the image of the invisible God, the firstborn over all creation. For by Him all things were created: things in heaven and on earth, visible and invisible, whether thrones or powers or rulers or authorities; all things were created by Him and for Him. He is before all things, and in him all things hold together. (Col. 1:15–17, NIV)

This reminded me that it was Christ who made me and who was holding me together during this walk through the valley of the shadow of death. With Him holding things together, I could be certain I would have the strength I needed day by day.

> The Lord is my Shepherd = That is Relationship!
> I shall not want = That is Supply!
> He makes me to lie down in green pastures = That is Rest!
> He leads me beside the still waters = That is Refreshment!
> He restores my soul = That is Healing!
> He leads me in the paths of righteousness = That is Guidance!
> For His name sake = That is Purpose!
> Yea, though I walk through the valley of the shadow of death = That is Testing!
> I will fear no evil = That is Protection!
> For You are with me = That is Faithfulness!
> Your rod and staff they comfort me = That is Discipline!
> You prepare a table before me in the presence of mine enemies = That is Hope!
> You anoint my head with oil = That is Consecration!
> My cup runs over = That is Abundance!

> Surely goodness and mercy shall follow me all the days of my life =
> That is Blessing!
> And I will dwell in the house of the Lord = That is Security!
> Forever = That is Eternity!
>
> —Unknown

The eternal home that is prepared for those who have accepted the sacrificial gift of Jesus as payment for their sins will be magnificent. During my season of radiation treatment, I started a group called Women Surviving Cancer under the Care of the Great Physician, and we gathered weekly in my home for tea and snacks but most of all for prayer and support. We were all persuaded that all things would work together for the good; even in the difficulties we were living, we could find some laughter and encouragement to brighten our valley experience. We came from all walks of life and had various types of cancer, but we joined together to look at what God's word had to say to encourage us. For a few weeks, we studied Randy Alcorn's book *Heaven*.[5]

The book provides reflection time on God's original design and handiwork in the Garden of Eden before the fall of humankind, when the created man and woman chose to disobey God's directive. As a result, not only did they and all their future prodigy suffer but also the whole creation was damaged. It had been a place with animals and humans living in perfect peace—green plants in various shades, delicious colorful fruit, and flowers growing without weeds. This is our promised true eternal home where we will experience the best of this world, from the multicolored sunsets over the ocean to the snowcapped peaks. We will be in awe when things are restored to their original design. The people will be filled with joy and laughter, and there will not be any fear or sadness. We will be constantly in the presence of the Lord where there is all the fruit of the spirit: love, joy, peace, patience, kindness, goodness, faithfulness, gentleness, and self-control (Gal. 5:22–23). There is no better place to be than heaven. Only after arriving on those shores will we be truly home.

Lord, thank you for leading me for your name's sake and healing me from the inside out. Thank you for putting the reminder of your sacrifice of love at the very foundation of every cell of my physical and spiritual being. You are keeping me from falling apart at the seams! I am persuaded that you have prepared an eternal home for me where I will always be in your presence and cease my wanderings.
Amen.

Notes

1. "Top Ten Most Read Books in the World," Visually, https://visual.ly/community/infographic/education/top-10-most-read-books-world.
2. Richard G. Stevens, "University of Connecticut," *Yakima Herald Republic*, October 9, 2017, 1A.
3. "Vitamin D Deficiency," Web MD, https://www.webmd.com/diet/guide/vitamin-d-deficiency#1.
4. Leo Giglio Talks about Laminin, YouTube video, 15:22, from the "How Great Is Our God" Tour posted by "candidickerson," September 2012, https://www.youtube.com/watch?v=iYFHQzLp4fM.
5. Randy Alcorn, *Heaven* (Carol Stream, IL: Tyndale House Publishers Inc., 2004).

CHAPTER 7

Are You Persuaded?

At the end of reasons comes persuasion.

—Ludwig Wittgenstein

Our minds can influence our moods, and in turn our moods can influence our thoughts. Together, they often determine our actions for better or worse. This interplay determines ultimately whether someone will fall apart under the burdens of anxiety, fear, and pain or become an overcomer and live an abundant life. Positive examples abound; one such is Lamaze breathing and relaxation techniques used to control the pain of labor and childbirth. Another example that is on the other end of the continuum of life is a highly trained psychoanalyst giving successful cognitive behavioral therapy to a despairing person on the roof of a ten-story building. Understanding the mind-body-spirit connection and the factors influencing decision making is a fascinating field of study.

Our decisions are a culmination of a plethora of interwoven factors, whether that decision is what cereal to purchase when there are fifteen varieties to choose from or whom to marry. We all know that decisions today will affect what happens in our lives tomorrow. There is a domino effect once our mind and emotions are set in motion that affects our physical health. Physicians have long recognized that there are more than physical influences affecting our health. The same medication given to two different people of the same size, gender, and age can affect them differently because human beings consist of far more than flesh and blood. The placebo effect alone can affect outcomes perceived by patients, based on multiple medical studies (meta-analysis) and presented in the *Annals of Internal Medicine.*[1] It was concluded that 95 percent of patients in a clinical study receiving intra-articular injections of placebo perceived an improvement despite not receiving an actual medication. Humans can be fooled.

When someone comes to a physician seeking true wellness, he or she is asking for something beyond just absence of disease. Wellness can be defined as "a dynamic state of health in which an individual progresses toward a higher level of functioning, achieving an optimum balance between internal and external environments."[2] Dr. Bill Hettler, cofounder of the National Wellness Institute (NWI), developed an interdependent model in 1976, commonly referred to as the Six Dimensions of Wellness, which includes the physical, emotional, occupational, social, intellectual, and spiritual dimensions.[3]

The scientific method requires a repeatable, observable phenomenon. This requirement can present problems. We can observe damage from high winds, but we cannot see the wind itself. The same applies to the warmth of the sun, gravity, and electricity. We can know when we are loved but cannot scientifically quantitate it. Even the best scientists are willing to accept that many things are beyond our ability to measure. Why would one person, despite multiple healthy lifestyle choices, still suffer from cancer, while someone else partaking of multiple toxic substances appears to be untouched? Could the factors determining ultimate health outcome be related to these other dimensions of wellness?

Curious scientific minds take a lot of persuasion—especially when things do not follow a logical progression—and I was no different. Years in the practice of medicine had their benefits when I found myself on my own search for the cause and cure of my cancer. I had friends who were pathologists, oncologists, surgeons, and radiologists. They supported me in my journey by calling or e-mailing, giving me their insights on my cancer diagnosis. I could also go online and research and interpret the latest studies, medications, and approaches. I had a surplus of data at my disposal. Sometimes I felt like I was drowning in a sea of information, but the primary groupings were three well-connected islands: mind, spirit, and physical dimensions.

Working on all three areas would improve my outcome, but I knew I needed to prioritize restoring physical health if I was going to have time to work on the other areas. Decisions regarding my physical care were challenging enough. At one point, I had five different oncology perspectives—and they were all different!

As I explored an official second opinion through the University of Washington Research Center in Seattle, I had a full team on board, which included an oncologist, a surgeon, a radiation oncologist, and a pharmacologist, all experts in the field of breast cancer engaged in an intellectually stimulating and professional dialogue with me. What a welcome discussion. The uninvited, cancerous breast tumor sat silently on my chest wall, waiting to learn its fate. It was clearly unchanged, despite more than two months of chemotherapy wreaking havoc on my veins, blood cells, and emotional heart. The final conclusion of the professionals: "Your type of cancer doesn't usually respond to chemotherapy." Unanimous agreement, but what were my options?

Second opinions and options are linked to second chances. We all like to know that if we fail the first time, we will be given another opportunity. We will have another practice, another game, another opportunity to win the battle. "If only I could do it again, I would..." or "If at first you don't succeed, try, try again." Just the idea of a whole team not giving up encouraged me. They had a plan.

They recommended completing the final few weeks of treatment as per the protocol and then proceeding with surgery. Just having an option other than chemo gave me some hope of light at the end of this very long tunnel of fatigue, hair loss, and loss of control over my day-by-day schedule. However, though my hometown oncologist agreed we were not making any progress in the battle, he was not persuaded by the second opinion. That day, he stopped the planned infusion of Taxol and started the big guns: three cycles of FAC (Fluorouracil, Adriamycin, and Cytoxan). He believed I should give this new chemotherapy concoction a chance to come out the victor.

The war was declared, and I felt the full brunt of this semiautomatic level regiment very quickly. I fell victim to dramatically increasing waves of nausea and fatigue, precipitously balanced with decreasing numbers of fighter white blood cells. These disappearing soldier blood cells would leave me vulnerable to a common viral or bacterial invader, which in turn could result in a rapid demise due to infection. Up to that point, I appeared to be strong and healthy, especially with my camouflage (wig) in place. I could focus on the needs of others during each shift I worked, which I know was psychologically beneficial as well. However, science long ago conclusively passed judgment on the emergency department setting as a microbiological incubator for some of the most virulent infectious diseases known to humankind. I was persuaded that it was time to hang up my white coat.

The white coat represents a professional commitment to our patients and our colleagues in the battle to save lives, and formal induction occurs in many medical schools around the world as students accept the challenges and don the cloak. The white coat represented my twenty years of service with comrades who were friends. To lose that role so abruptly and unwillingly was a source of occupational and emotional grief. However, time was of the essence, and I would need to focus on surviving the onslaught of the drugs rather than grieving the loss.

I lost innumerable days lying around in bed due to complete exhaustion. Accomplishing one task a day was all I could hope for in the initial two weeks, with only a brief five-day hiatus before the next round. It was like being hit by waves, breaker after breaker, on the California coast. I found myself lying around nearly lifeless; however, it was my previous experience of teaching in China that was a source of direction to me and a new weapon in my armory.

Acupuncture definitely gave respite during this battle. After round two of the more toxic chemo, I called on the aid of my friend and local certified acupuncturist Johanna Liu. Medical research supports this adjunct to cancer therapy,[4] and I was willing to try anything to regain my stamina and control the nausea. Though I could not begin to explain how this process worked, I was persuaded that it did through my personal experience. Somehow, the tiny needles in my right ear, arm, and leg and the hot suction cups on my back seemed to put me to sleep and helped me detoxify from the chemicals, so I could function fairly well until the next round of treatment. I could not observe or reproduce the changes, but I know they were real, as I found a new surge of energy and appetite within a half hour.

Persuasion. *Merriam-Webster* defines "persuasion" as "an opinion held with complete assurance."[5] Through my more than four decades on planet earth, I had become persuaded of many things. One decision, however, stood above all others and would dramatically affect all my subsequent decisions.

"How does that happen?" "Why does that work that way?" I always seemed to be looking for some answer. As I entered my teenage years, I had various biology classes that helped me explore answers to some of these questions and other classes to help me to explore beyond to the proverbial question "What is truth?" I found the philosophies of this world and our existence to be fascinating. Plato and Aristotle had their system of beliefs. Hinduism, Confucianism, and Buddhism had very different ways to a peaceful life. I was overwhelmed with the variety of world religions. Though I had been raised in the United States, where our predominant religion was Christianity, this curious teenage mind still needed to explore the frontier for itself.

I had been raised in the rapidly growing community of Orange County, California. Navel orange trees abounded, and the local soil produced most of the world's sweetest, most vibrant red strawberries. With the surplus of fresh fruits and vegetables in this sun-drenched part of the world, I did not feel physical hunger, but deep within me, a spiritual hunger was growing. In my early childhood years, we would attend church on an occasional Christmas or Easter Sunday. It was confusing to me at the time because I thought that all they ever talked about was either Jesus being born or him dying on the cross. I never heard stories of his life. Attending church on these holidays seemed to appease the cultural expectations—it seemed the American thing to do, but it left me wanting. Home discussions about religion and philosophy were not a part of my childhood years. My parents did not express their faith openly or incorporate religious activities, except perhaps a prayer at our Thanksgiving meal. My father was more focused on finding work as an aerospace engineer at the time our nation was challenged in its "race for space."

As the United States was on its search for the means to place a man on the moon, I was at the beginning of a search to know the One who made the moon. I was still quite confused about what this life was all about, what it all meant to me, and my purpose for living. Were we just puppets on the strings of a cosmic puppeteer, or was there some other design in placing humans at the top of the pecking order of life organisms? Were we actually designed for an ultimate purpose, or did we begin as a bacterium in some galactic swamp? How would these answers I sought affect me on a daily basis? Despite studying about Darwin's theory of evolution in my biology classes, I was not persuaded. In fact, in his own writings, he said that if there were a lack of transitional species, then his theory should be abandoned. In more than one hundred years of archeological digs, only one set of bones could be considered transitional support—not the billions that would need to take the human race from a one-cell bacterium to a complex organism able to send neurological signals faster than anything man could design.

My brief introduction to Christianity left me with a lot of unanswered questions and wanting more knowledge about this religion that influenced people all around the world. Even though it was almost two thousand years ago, people were so persuaded of its truth that they were willing to die for their founder rather than deny their faith. Martyrs were plentiful, estimated in the hundreds daily, with more than three hundred prayer requests per day worldwide to one agency alone.[6] Missionaries had been spread all around the globe to tell others about their faith, leaving loved ones behind.

The book *Through Gates of Splendor* by Elisabeth Elliot affected me greatly on a personal level. In 1956 five young men, including Elliot's husband, Jim, traveled into the jungles of Ecuador to establish communication with the fierce Huaorani Tribe, a people whose only previous response to the outside world had been to attack all strangers. The men's mission combined modern technology with innate ingenuity, sparked by a passionate determination to get the gospel to those without Christ. In a nearby village, their wives waited to hear from them. The news they received—all five missionaries had been murdered—changed lives around the world forever. Elisabeth chose to return to the tribe with her son and helped them during their measles epidemic. The tribe came to understand the forgiveness of God through her persistence and personal sacrifice.[7]

What was so attractive that a person would be willing to surrender his or her life for the cause of Christ? Fortunately, I had a lead to possible answers. Some friends at school spoke often of going to church—more than just once or twice a year—in fact, once or twice a week. What did they talk about those other weeks of the year? I was curious.

There was one thing I was persuaded of as a scrawny, acne-afflicted fifteen-year-old. I was not the heartthrob of any of the young men I had my eyes on. No winks, no dances, no dates. When I was invited by a girlfriend to some youth activities at a Nazarene church close to my house, I was intrigued by what she said they did. Their pizza party nights, weeklong summer camping trips, boating on lakes, and midwinter snow retreats sounded like a lot of fun, and that could have been enough of a magnet for the average teenager. In all honesty, the greater attraction was that my high-school girlfriends had captured some very handsome boyfriends at church. Perhaps there I could find the answer to my ultimate search for true love, my soul mate.

This search for love seems to be universal. It is there in all the culturally diverse countries I have traveled during the past forty years. It is a common desire of people, whether they are living in the traditional, ornate, porcelain-filled tea houses of China or the mud-covered, thatched-roof shacks in remote areas of Africa, to be completely known and to be completely loved. Unconditionally. No strings attached. It was something that could not be bought or sold. It was more than just a sexual encounter. It was true intimacy. Some search for it in human relationships, over and over again. Some give up the search entirely after their first failed attempt. I was still young and naïve, so I thought I would try once again.

In those weeknight gatherings, there was usually some fun activity like ping pong and then a short Bible study, in which they talked about what Jesus did on the rest of those days between birth and death, how his documented responses to stressful life events might apply to our lives. The meeting consistently ended in a prayer, and that was where I was most mesmerized. I was intrigued by how science-minded peers of mine could confidently speak into the air a prayer to a God they could not see. How could they believe in someone they could not see? How would one start a relationship with a power greater than him- or herself? How could they be certain anyone was listening? A lot of questions swirled around my curious mind, but some things were certain. In those meetings, I sensed a peaceful presence and felt at home. I felt the leaders had a sincere desire for me to be there and also to know this God they spoke of frequently. They were extremely kind, loving, and forgiving to all the kids who attended. I kept coming back.

I also started my own "research." In 1972 Josh McDowell's *Evidence That Demands a Verdict*[8] was published. As a young man, McDowell considered himself an agnostic. He truly believed that Christianity was worthless. However, when challenged to intellectually examine the claims of Christianity, Josh discovered compelling, overwhelming evidence for the reliability of the Christian faith. In this book, there were chapters on the uniqueness and reliability of the Bible with evidence from secular historians, anthropologists, and various other science-based experts who studied the claims of Christianity. The conclusions were as follows:

- Jesus actually lived and claimed to be God.
- His claims were so clear the Jewish people were willing to kill Him for blasphemy.
- He not only died, but His death was also confirmed by Roman soldiers who did crucifixions daily.
- His tomb was guarded by a troop of Roman soldiers who would be killed if the body were stolen.
- No evidence of the bones of Jesus were ever found, though many eyewitnesses could identify where He was placed after being removed from the cross and wrapped in pounds of cloth and ointments.

If the evidence is true, and He rose from the dead like He said He would, that should get our attention. No one has ever done that. Not Confucius, Buddha, Mohammed, or any other well-recognized spiritual leader. None of them claimed to die in my place for the sins I had committed. Though young, I knew there were things that I had already said and done that were not right, and it left a tight knot of guilt and lack of peace in my inner soul. I had to come to terms with my personal verdict on the evidence.

On one bright Sunday morning in 1973, the pastor of the small church I had started to attend gave a clear message on heaven and asked whether we could answer with assurance: "Should you die tonight, are you persuaded you would enter heaven?" As a teenager, I had not considered that question, but I knew at that moment I did not feel ready to die. If I should die, how would I know if I would go to the place called heaven, which was described as a peaceful garden with Jesus, or whether I would go to an eternal destination called hell, where there would be endless torment, physical and emotional? How could people have that assurance? The pastor explained that all people do things they know are wrong. Now, that I had to agree with! Though I had not done things I had heard about on the news, like killings, or acts those fictional characters performed in the horror movies I viewed as a child, I could relate to actions, words, and thoughts that were not loving and not like what Jesus did during His life on earth. The Bible calls this sin, and it is inherent in all humans because of a sinful nature. This nature had its origins in the original humans, Adam and Eve. God had designed them for a relationship with Him, placed them in a beautiful garden, and given them a choice to obey or disobey and bear the consequences of death and separation from God.

They chose disobedience, and the rest is history. Ever since, all humans have had a rebellious bent in which our head knowledge and actions do not line up. I, too, would have a tendency to choose to do wrong, and this would separate me from a holy and perfect God. I could accept a pardon being presented by a perfect God to His disobedient children. It was my choice. However, where I spent eternity, heaven or hell, was dependent on my willingness to accept the work of His perfect Son, Jesus, who died on the cross in payment, a blood ransom for my choices. One who is holy, dying sacrificially to make the unrighteous righteous. To not accept Jesus and to believe there was another way was to say that Jesus's sacrifice of love demonstrated on that painful cross was in vain, a waste. In arrogance, I would be saying that my feeble attempt to be good based on the method of my choosing would have to be acceptable for a holy God.

His sacrificial love to restore an intimate relationship tugged at my heartstrings. It was my choice to believe His exclusive way. Jesus had said He alone was the way, the truth, and the life. No one would have a relationship with the Heavenly Father if he or she was not willing to accept His sacrificial gift. Contrary to what some world religions and philosophies purported, there were not many ways to be acceptable to God, and I could not work hard enough in my humanness to please a holy God. He chose His Son's sacrifice as the way to please Him. We each have the opportunity to accept or reject the gift. A pardon being extended to a prisoner doomed to public execution must be accepted, or the prisoner will still face death. Once the penalty has been paid or the pardon accepted, the prisoner walks free. Jesus's death on the cross paid the price.

That day, I was persuaded. That gift of sacrifice for my guilt was enough for me and enough for God. I was overwhelmed with peace, and I knew I was accepted and loved unconditionally. I was never the same. Early on in the quest to learn more about Jesus, I devoured large sections of the Bible, reading for hours at a time, and tried to understand Jesus and His promises to me. As I meditated on a few verses, they sank deep into my soul, and they would be the foundation for fearless travels and adventures in the days to come.

> For I am persuaded, that neither death, nor life, nor angels, nor principalities, nor powers, nor things present, nor things to come, nor height, nor depth, nor any other creature shall be able to separate us from the love of God, which is in Christ Jesus our Lord. (Rom. 8:38–39, NIV)

Years later, during the storms of cancer, I was reminded of my persuasion that neither death nor life (neither chemo nor cancer) could separate me from the love of God, which is in Christ Jesus our Lord. I knew that, though anxiety over death might come to choke me at times, for me to live was Christ and to die was gain (Phil. 1:21). I was in a win-win situation—continue life on earth to bring glory to God or enter heaven where the joys would overwhelm me in the continual presence of the Lord. I could rest knowing that the love of God would keep me in the center of His will, and He would never leave me or forsake me. The cross was the ultimate and only demonstration of unconditional love I would ever need. No other miracle was needed.

In the book *What Cancer Cannot Do*, Phyllis Ten Elshof compiled the writings of many cancer patients under the following chapter titles:

It cannot cripple God's love
It cannot shatter hope
It cannot corrode faith
It cannot destroy peace
It cannot kill friendship
It cannot shut out memories
It cannot silence courage
It cannot invade the soul
It cannot steal eternal life
It cannot conquer the spirit

"I am the Lord, the God of all mankind. Is anything too hard for me" (Jer. 32:27, NIV).

Dear Lord,

Thank you for persuading me of Your love, regardless of my circumstances, and that by Your power, the most important things in life cannot be taken away from me. Your love has taken away the fear of death, and I will always have hope, faith, peace, friendship, memories, courage, and ultimately Your Spirit to remind me of eternal life. Amen.

Notes

1. Raveendhara R. Bannuru, Timothy E. McAlindon, Matthew C. Sullivan, John B. Wong, David M. Kent, and Christopher H. Schmid, "Effectiveness and Implications of Alternative Placebo Treatments: A Systematic Review and Network Meta-Analysis of Osteoarthritis Trials," *Annals of Internal Medicine* 163 (2015): 365–72, http://annals.org/aim/article-abstract/2398908/

effectiveness-implications-alternative-placebo-treatments-systematic-review-network-meta-analysis?doi=10.7326%2fM15-0623#, doi: 10.7326/M15-0623.
2. *Mosby's Medical Dictionary*, 9th ed., s.v. "wellness."
3. National Wellness Institute, "The Six Dimensions of Wellness, http://www.nationalwellness.org/?page=Six_Dimensions.
4. F. Z. Zia, O. Olaku, T. Bao, A. Berger, G. Deng, A. Yin Fan, M. K. Garcia, P. M. Herman, T. J. Kaptchuk, E. J. Ladas, H. M. Langevin, L. Lao, W. Lu, V. Napadow, R. C. Niemtzow, A. J. Vickers, X. Shelley Wang, C. M. Witt, and J. J. Mao, "The National Cancer Institute's Conference on Acupuncture for Symptom Management in Oncology: State of the Science, Evidence, and Research Gaps," *Journal of the National Cancer Institute Monographs* 25 (2017), doi: 10.1093/jncimonographs/lgx005.
5. https://www.merriam-webster.com/dictionary/persuasion.
6. The Voice of the Martyrs, https://secure.persecution.com/radio/.
7. Elisabeth Elliott, *Through Gates of Splendor* (Carol Stream, IL: Tyndale House Publishers Inc., 1956).
8. Josh McDowell, *Evidence That Demands a Verdict: Life-Changing Truth for a Skeptical World* (San Bernadino, CA, Campus Crusade for Life, International Publishers, 1972, 2017).

CHAPTER 8

Courage for Tomorrow

COURAGE WAS NEEDED FOR THE next step in my journey toward healing. Nelson Mandela, a South African political leader who had spent twenty-seven years imprisoned for his effort to improve his country, spoke on courage. Upon his release, he declared, "I learned that courage was not the absence of fear, but the triumph over it. The brave man is not he who does not feel afraid, but he who conquers that fear."

I could not be courageous without first comprehending the greatness of the problem. The reality was that the lobular breast cancer I had was extremely resistant to four different chemotherapies. The second trial of chemo did not change the hardness or size of the tumor. Chemotherapeutic options were exhausted, and so was I. Surgery was the next step traditional cancer treatment had to offer. Prior to taking the next step to mastectomy, I chose to enjoy a swim with the dolphins in Orlando, Florida.

There was something very healing about catching a ride on a smiling dolphin's back after years of my childhood highlighted by watching *Flipper*, a series about a boy's pet dolphin. Holding on to Roxy, my appointed dolphin ride, was magical, and I could not help letting out a good laugh. The warm water and beautiful setting of Discovery Cove allowed me to snorkel with the tropical fish and sit under a cool, refreshing mini waterfall. Being with my dear friend and prayer warrior, Diane, playing like we were kids again, refreshed my body, mind, and spirit. Diane is the kind of balanced friend who can make me laugh and make me pray for courage.

"A happy heart is good medicine and a cheerful mind works healing, but a broken spirit dries up the bones" (Prov. 17:22, AMP). True wisdom uttered by Solomon thousands of years ago. Laughter pours out of a happy heart, but what does that actually do?

The therapeutic value of laughter in medicine was recently reviewed by Dr. Ramon Mora-Ripoll from Barcelona, Spain. Dr. Mora-Ripoll reviewed many research articles to identify, critically evaluate, and summarize the literature related to laughter, medicine, and health care. His conclusions showed laughter has physiological, psychological, social, spiritual, and quality-of-life benefits. Therapeutic efficacy is derived from spontaneous and self-induced laughter, occurring both with and without humor. The brain is not able to distinguish between these types. Although there is not enough data to demonstrate that laughter is an all-round healing agent, this review concludes that sufficient evidence exists to suggest that laughter has some positive, quantifiable effects on certain aspects of health.[1]

The Mayo Clinic has also reported on both short-term and long-term effects of humor and laughter.[2] Short-term benefits of laughter include the following:

1. It stimulates organs; enhances intake of oxygen-rich air; stimulates the heart, lungs, and muscles; and increases the endorphins (feel-good hormones) released by your brain.
2. It activates and relieves your stress response.
3. It soothes tension as it stimulates circulation and aids in muscle relaxation.

Long-term benefits include the following:

1. Laughter improves your immune system. Negative thoughts manifest into chemical reactions that can affect your body by bringing more stress into your system and decreasing your immunity. In contrast, positive thoughts can actually release neuropeptides that help fight stress and potentially more serious illnesses.

2. It relieves pain. Laughter may ease pain by causing the body to produce its own natural painkillers.
3. It increases personal satisfaction. Laughter can make it easier to cope with difficult situations. It also helps you connect with other people.
4. It improves mood. Many people experience depression, sometimes due to chronic illness. Laughter can help lessen depression and anxiety.

After frolicking with the dolphins, I returned to my home state and wrapped my body in a blue-printed hospital gown, hearing the clicking of the gurney wheels rolling toward the operating table. My mind was still hopeful. I still held a committed belief that a miracle would take place and that the surgeon would tell me the tumor had resolved and was not to be found. I had heard about such cases. I certainly was not lacking in desire or an assurance that with God all things were possible. I had seen the miraculous happen with my patients multiple times in my career, such as people being shocked back to life. However, as the anesthesia lifted, and I awoke with intense pain, the draining chest tube and bandages confirmed reality. I knew the miracle I had wanted had not happened. I was encouraged to get news that no spread of the cancerous tumor had been found in the sentinel lymph node, that first place the cancer would have spread if it was going to start its journey to other places in the body. I was free of cancer. That was worth celebrating.

However, one week later, as I sat on the exam table, the surgeon read the official pathology report: "Sentinel node positive for carcinoma, malignancy noted up to the margin of the breast specimen in multiple locations." He also told me there were no indications of necrosis (tumor cell death), despite the four chemo agents. My courage and faith were severely tested at that point. Based on initial scans, this new information would suggest that despite treatment with four powerful chemo drugs for four months, the cancer had continued to grow into lymph-node tissue. It not only survived but also thrived in the toxic environment that flowed through my veins. Despite the Seattle cancer center's most aggressive surgical intervention, microscopic cancer cells persisted in the skin cells that were left behind. In fact, cancer that very second was multiplying throughout the highway system of the lymphatics that flowed to every far-reaching corner of my body. When it multiplied enough to be noticed, would it be more resistant than before? Even less amenable to intervention and cure?

As I walked out to the surgeon's waiting room, my eyes found my mother in the reception area. I glanced into her eyes but had to look away. We are told that eyes are the window to our souls. People who are good at reading eyes, like law enforcement and detectives, can clearly tell if someone is telling the truth or being dishonest. Moms are experts with their children, no matter what their ages, in recognizing pain and concern. I was not ready to tell her the news. I knew it would require me to find courage within myself first. This news would dash her hope that I could close this cancer chapter of my life forever.

I knew that before I could encourage anyone, I needed to spend time alone with my Great Physician to receive His prognosis and the courage only He could infuse. In times of desperation, I have found Him to meet me and to speak to me through various Bible verses and bring a peace that passes understanding. Typically, I read one chapter at a time in a methodical and progressive way. On that day, things were different. I randomly opened my Bible toward the middle (Bible roulette) and cried out to God, "Please, speak to me!" The questions swirled, and I needed answers. How was I to live now, in light of this new information? How could I comfort my friends and family with any assurance, knowing what I now had to accept? How much more time did I have? How should I prioritize my limited days?

As my eyes fell on the open text, Psalm 118:1, I knew I had started in a good place. I read, "Give thanks to the Lord for He is good, His love endures forever." That took me back to what I had been persuaded about when I had started my journey with him about twenty-five years before; nothing would separate me from his love.

Reading further in that chapter, a few verses seemed to jump out at me as if they were in bold print, highlighted and underlined with my name on them: "I will not die, but live and proclaim what the Lord has done. The Lord has chastened me severely but he has not given me over to death" (Ps. 118:17–18, NIV).

I rubbed my eyes and read again, but the words were unchanged. The undeniable peace fell like a heavy blanket on a cold winter day. It was a spiritual prognosis and prescription from my Great Physician. Though I know that someday I will die, He was clearly telling me I had a job to do, to proclaim what He had done for me. I wondered what that proclaiming would involve.

Over the next few weeks, life became a blur. In the midst of healing from surgery, I was being assessed by a multitude of doctors and technicians to prepare me for radiation to my chest wall. It was decided, in light of the tenacity of this cancer, that I would initiate treatment three weeks earlier than usual: maximum radiation to all zones of the lymph nodes in or around the tumor site. I was now working strategy number four to obliterate the stealthy intruder.

Radiation oncologists have a hard job. Most of their patients come for palliative care, meaning that they shrink tumors to relieve pain in a dying person. Their work is usually not curative but at times, like in my case, can be preventative in spread of cancer. Most of the patients sitting with me in the waiting room were stage 4, meaning the tumors they had were progressive even beyond the immediate lymph nodes to more distant organs, such as the bones, liver, or brain. It was difficult to feel hopeful in this company of fellow patients, and no one was laughing.

Hope was lost as I looked into the eyes of these oncologists I had worked with as a physician. Their awkward smiles belied what I could read in their eyes. No secrets could be held back, and they diverted their gazes from me frequently. They spoke of the treatment plan, not of hope. The facts flowed: thirty-three sessions, administered five days a week in fifteen-minute appointments. A burn to the chest would slow things down. It was critical not to miss a session. My strong faith in the spiritual prescription I had received just weeks earlier began to wither like a blade of grass in a desert terrain, longing for a single drop of water. In that desperate moment, I remembered a spiritual prescription I had offered to others so many times, either as a physician or a fellow patient. I sought prayer with my friend Diane, who knew how to call out to God. I also sought for a dose of refreshing hope. I found myself returning to a prayer room where volunteers who were people of faith would gather and pray for those in need on a rotational basis. I had been there before, but obviously, things were not better. I would give this new group of prayer warriors a chance to restore my hope in the God of miracles.

On that warm August day in the state of Washington, this small group of strangers gathered around me in response to my request for prayer because of cancer. I did not need to elaborate; I would leave them to do the work they knew best. As they began to pray, one woman stopped and told me she had a "word from the Lord." She asked if I would like to hear it.

"Yes!" I said adamantly.

She opened her Bible and began to read: "I will not die, but live and proclaim what the Lord has done. The Lord has chastened me severely but He has not given me over to death" (Ps. 118:17–18).

Only my Great Physician could speak truth into my life to give me hope in my hour of weakness. Only He could whisper that same truth into the ears of a faithful prayer warrior to encourage me. For a scientific mind, that event alone would defy statistical probability: that a total stranger would give me such significant verses when there are more than sixty-six books in the Bible and thousands of verses. That encouraging day will always remain fresh in my heart and my soul. Though my body would always remain under the curse or threat of cancer, it was well with my soul. I could choose to fix my eyes on the job of proclaiming what He had done for me.

In Your Darkest Hour, Have You Been Able to Say, "It Is Well with My Soul"?

In the historical accounting of the famous hymn "It Is Well with My Soul," we have insight into a trying time in author Horatio Spafford's life. In November 1873, he had barely recovered from the death of his four-year-old son and the Great Chicago Fire that had devastated him financially. He sent his wife and four daughters on the French ship *Ville du Havre* for a vacation in France as he finished up business, planning to set sail a few days later. Somewhere in the Atlantic, the *Ville du Havre* collided with a British ship coming the other way, and it sank in twelve minutes. His daughters perished; only his wife survived.

Spafford took the next ship he could find, and as he passed the spot where the *Ville du Havre* had gone down, he began to pen the following words, later set to music by his good friend Philip Bliss:

When peace, like a river, attendeth my way,
When sorrows like sea billows roll;
Whatever my lot, Thou hast taught me to say,
It is well, it is well with my soul.

It is well with my soul,
It is well, it is well with my soul.

Though Satan should buffet, though trials should come,
Let this blest assurance control,
That Christ hath regarded my helpless estate,
And hath shed His own blood for my soul.

My sin—oh, the bliss of this glorious thought!
My sin, not in part but the whole,
Is nailed to the cross, and I bear it no more,
Praise the Lord, praise the Lord, O my soul!

For me, be it Christ, be it Christ hence to live:
If Jordan above me shall roll,
No pang shall be mine, for in death as in life
Thou wilt whisper Thy peace to my soul.

But, Lord, 'tis for Thee, for Thy coming we wait,
The sky, not the grave, is our goal;
Oh, trump of the angel! Oh, voice of the Lord!
Blessed hope, blessed rest of my soul!

And Lord, haste the day when the faith shall be sight,
The clouds be rolled back as a scroll;
The trump shall resound, and the Lord shall descend,
Even so, it is well with my soul.[3]

Now living in the AD (after diagnosis) phase, I had a choice. I could choose to be myopic, focusing on the world of cancer and how it tried to invade my plans, dreams, and time—how it filled my days with appointments, deforming surgery, nausea, and lifelessness beneath a beam of daily radiation. My other choice was to be grateful for the day I had. During a time of reflection, I penned these thoughts:

Living one day at a time

The dirt clods on the dark casket were just a dream, and I have been resurrected to a new beginning. How would I live again?

As the sun would rise, I would start my day by talking to the Giver of life, who would fill me with His love, so grateful for the gift of life itself that overflows with possibilities.

In the light of the morning, I would fill my family's basket with gifts of love, laughter, and encouragement for their daily journey—love as a soothing sunscreen to protect them prophylactically against the world's burning rays of painful words and action. I would dose them generously with tears of laughter to provide oil of gladness for their sorrow and give a loud cheering encouragement to dispel despair and give them the strength to reach their finish line and hear "well done."

In the noontime sun, I would look beyond my home walls to the needs in my neighbor's life. Is there a well-watered flower basket of joy I can bring to them that day that can be a lasting seed of harvest in the days to come?

As the day marched on, I would join with other soldiers to gift the world for better, not for worse. Would it be a cure for cancer, a joyful dance, or a smile of hope for a stranger? No gift would be too large or small. Is there a lonely one I can comfort, one lost that could be found? A lighthouse of direction needed in a storm? I would seek for empty, needy baskets that could be filled with gifts of love.

As the sun would drop from the horizon, I would drop to my knees, talking to the Giver, so grateful for the gift of life itself that overflowed with possibilities. As darkness would fall, I would have one final request—another opportunity to live one day at a time.

Each day became another opportunity to live courageously one day at a time and choose a telescopic focus on God and his plans for me. Looking back on that season of my life, I see clearly that God's lens for my AD chapter was filled with a kaleidoscope of blessings and adventures. By His grace during the four years after my cancer diagnosis, between 2008 and 2012, I had the following opportunities:

- Shared my testimony of cancer with more than nine hundred people at my church and many other churches in Washington;
- Spoke at various Be Still retreats in the Pacific Northwest;
- Watched my daughter Faith graduate from college, get married, and start her career as an actuary;
- Watched my daughter Serena graduate from high school and college;
- Celebrated my mother's eightieth birthday;
- Became a professor at a medical school in Washington in 2009;
- Climbed a bubbling, red-hot active volcano in Guatemala in 2009;
- Swam the Columbia River from the Pasco bank to the Kennewick bank in 2009;
- Led Partners for Life in an emergency training in China in 2009;
- Celebrated with Spain after their World Cup Soccer victory in 2010;
- Encouraged those in cancer treatment in Mongolia in 2010;
- Treated babies with AIDS in Guinea-Bissau and helped with the country's wound-care clinic development in 2011;
- Taught US medical students in needy settings in Guatemala, Venezuela, and the Philippines;

- Medically and spiritually treated women from the brothels of Nicaragua in 2012;
- Zip-lined through the Redwood Forest in California in 2012;
- Kayaked with the sea lions in California in 2012; and
- Moved to Zambia, Africa, in December 2012. (More in the next chapter!)

Thank You, Lord. With you all things are possible. You have given me courage to do things beyond my capabilities. It is well with my soul, and You are giving me telescopic vision for the future in Africa! Amen.

Notes

1. Ramon Mora-Ripoli, "The Therapeutic Value of Laughter in Medicine, *Alternative Therapies in Health and Medicine* 16(6) (2010): 56–64.
2. "Stress Management," Mayo Clinic, https://www.mayoclinic.org/healthy-lifestyle/stress-management/in-depth/stress-relief/art-20044456?pg=1.
3. Gena Philibert-Ortega, "'It Is Well with My Soul': The Story of Horatio Spafford," blog post, February 5, 2015, https://blog.genealogybank.com/it-is-well-with-my-soul-the-story-of-horatio-spafford.html.

CHAPTER 9

Where Is Zambia?

DESTINATION: ZAMBIA, AFRICA. WHAT BETTER day to depart to my new home than 12/12/12? As I deplaned onto the black tarmac at the sparse, warm airport, I wondered, "How did I find myself clear on the other side of the globe?" The answer was clear: divinely guided step after step, similar to how he encouraged me throughout my cancer journey and in the days that followed.

After recovering from the cancer year of 2008, I looked forward to returning to my work in the emergency department. My life had slowed down in 2008, and I had invested in reflection and relationships. As I returned to the hustle and bustle of the ED, I somehow did not feel I fit into that oh-so-familiar setting. Somehow, my passion for efficiency and speed was diminished. I had a growing passion to teach the prevention of disease.

Since starting as a professor and the medical director at Columbia Basin College in 2000, I had experienced joy in seeing students start their journey of learning about human anatomy and end up saving multiple lives every day. EMS personnel are my heroes, and I deeply respect the hard work they do to keep people alive. I considered it a privilege to teach them to save lives.

In 2008 I was asked to share my experience of starting Grace Clinic at Pacific Northwest University (PNWU), a new osteopathic medical school in Yakima, Washington. Through that first exposure and subsequent opportunities to engage with the faculty and dean, I found myself employed in a part-time position by the fall of 2009, teaching clinical skills. Preclinical skills are needed for doctors in training to prepare them to obtain a history, perform an examination, and process the data collected into a diagnosis and plan. These are introduced prior to their first patient encounter.

Working with that very first class of frontier-spirited students stirred a passion within me that gave me a boost of energy and clear purpose. I found it invigorating and a wonderful opportunity to share the "pearls of the trade" that came from years of experience with patient care, first as a nurse and then as a physician. Though I continued to work in the emergency department, I found my heart invested in the work at PNWU. My hours were increased in 2010, and I was able to join a group of medical students when they went to Guatemala to help with clinic work for a few weeks. By 2011, I was focused full-time on clinical-skills training at the medical school and had left my work in the emergency department. I was also able to work at the Union Gospel Mission clinic with students and take another group of students to the Philippines to supervise their exposure to medical care in resource-limited environments. In both of those settings, my experience with domestic and international work with the needy was very useful.

During those years of academic medicine, I was challenged to consider various methodologies to make the classes more interesting. Various patient role-plays and small group activities based on some of my own real-life scenarios made the training a lot of fun. I was even able to help the students stage disaster drills with the local fire department, like I had done while traveling with Partners for Life. Various skills I had performed as a nurse for years, such as the placement of intravenous and Foley bladder catheters, were easy for me to teach to these fledgling health-care providers. These young doctors would be better prepared as team players in patient care, understanding what each member of the team was doing and how they might be able to assist as needed. Though holistic care was introduced, it was at a very basic level, which left me wanting to teach more in that area. In this secular US academic setting, not everyone appreciated the intricately woven spiritual components that would manifest with nearly every future patient encounter.

In November 2011, I had another of what I call my "verily, verily" experiences. What I have found in reading the Bible through the years is that when Jesus spoke, he often said, "Verily, verily, I say to you" (also translated as "truly, truly") to emphasize the point he was making. In my life, when two very similar events happen in close proximity, I pay attention. Though the Bible, God's word, is powerful in helping us understand God's desire and general direction for us, at times the Holy Spirit will speak specifically to us through various experiences or deep within our souls to help direct us in the course we need to travel. Certainly, I would never find "Go to Zambia" in the Bible, so the Lord used other experiences to ensure I would be following him to the destination of his choosing.

A friend of mine who graduated from medical school with me, Dr. Don Adema, knew of my interest in teaching medical students internationally. He had a patient who was leaving for Zambia and shared the work he would be doing with a startup Christian university. This patient had sent him a link to a site showing the need there, and Dr. Don felt prompted to forward it to me. Included in the information was the need for physicians to teach in a medical school in Lusaka. At the time, I thought it might be a good thing to do for a few weeks over the next summer break, but I did not have much time to focus on something more than seven months away in the midst of my busy schedule. Two days later, though, my daughter came for a visit and suggested we watch a movie called *Faith Like Potatoes*. The opening line of the movie said, "Filmed in Zambia."

Why was I suddenly hearing about Zambia twice in just a few days? Where was Zambia? I Googled a map and found it on the southern African continent and then went back to the e-mail that linked to the director of African Christian University (ACU), Dr. Ken Turnbull. I sent a message with my resume attached, expressing an interest in hearing more about the need and how I might possibly be helpful. I mentioned I would be available for a few weeks the next summer.

After a Skype conversation with Ken the following week, he asked if I would pray about being involved in the start of a Christian medical school. Obviously, that was more than just a request for a few weeks of service. That would require a possible move at some point, and I needed to know if this was direction from the Lord. I told him I would pray about it and called on my prayer warriors to join with me in a forty-day commitment to pray and seek the Lord's will on this next step.

Forty days is a number found in many places in the Bible; it rained for forty days in Noah's time, manna (food) was provided to the Israelites for forty years, Moses sought the Lord on the mountain for forty days and nights, but most significant to me, Jesus fasted for forty days and nights in the desert before starting His ministry (Matt. 4:2). I remembered I had encouraged the same time of prayer with the small planning group for Grace Clinic. We were all blessed with the God-glorifying results of that ministry.

By mid-December 2011, just a few weeks into our season of prayer, I was already seeing some signs of confirmation and answers to my prayers. One request I had of the Lord was that a vacant rental house of mine would sell. The Realtor reminded me that we were going into our cold Washington state winter and holiday season. This was the worst time to sell. Furthermore, because of the international financial crisis, the real-estate market was at its lowest point in many years. As a step of faith, I suggested on asking a price of $3,000 more than she recommended and an open house, also something that she said was not typically productive.

In December, after one open house on a snowy day, I had my full asking price from a pastor and his family who had been "looking for that house for ten years." They were the only ones who saw the house, and the deal closed within six weeks. When God wants us to be assured of His leading, even slow real-estate markets and snowstorms dare not stand in the way of His plan!

In the midst of that prayer season, seeking clarification on Zambia, I was struck with a need in Managua, Nicaragua. I had learned that children were sold into prostitution, and this just tore at my heart. In January 2012, I was able to assist a team of doctors from the Christian Medical and Dental Association in medically screening vulnerable women and their children who had been involved in human trafficking. Some of the children had been sold by their mothers for only five dollars to help buy food or other needed supplies. It was a very emotional but rewarding week, bringing some of them to the safe house and seeing them make choices to leave behind their pasts and begin new lives. At House of Hope, they were able to learn some skills that could eventually help them support themselves outside prostitution. At the end of the week, the team joined in worship, thanking the Lord for the good work we were able to accomplish. And this song would become very significant in my guidance.

The lyrics to the song "Here I Am, Lord," by James Kilbane:

I, the Lord of sea and sky,
I have heard My people cry.
All who dwell in dark and sin,
My hand will save.
I who made the stars of night,

I will make their darkness bright.
Who will bear My light to them?
Whom shall I send?

Here I am Lord, Is it I Lord?
I have heard You calling in the night.
I will go Lord, if You lead me.
I will hold Your people in my heart.
I, the Lord of snow and rain,
I have borne by people's pain
I have wept for love of them
They turn away.

I will break their hearts of stone,
Give them hearts for love alone.
I will speak My word to them,
Whom shall I send?

I, the Lord of wind and flame,
I will tend the poor and lame
I will set a feast for them,
My hand will save.
Finest bread I will provide,
Till their hearts be satisfied.
I will give My life to them,
Whom shall I send?

It was a song that struck the core of my very soul. I fell on my knees in surrender. I knew the Lord was saying, "Yes, I do want you to go," and I needed to surrender to Him no matter the cost. The Bible teaches us in many places that the righteous are to walk by faith and not by sight. Now was my moment to live what I believed. I returned from that trip and gave notice of my intent to leave in six months to my employer at the beautiful new PNWU medical school. Though I had not been to Zambia, I was persuaded I should move there.

What I find exciting on the adventure of trusting God is that He often asks me to do something that defies reason, something outside logical scientific progression. Simply because of His perspective on the past, present, and future, I must acknowledge my limitations and choose to obey. I know I am lacking in all understanding, especially of the future perspective.

In the midst of preparing myself for a May 2012 departure to Zambia, I also felt prompted to purchase a condo in San Diego, California. This, of course, did not make any logical sense. In obedience, on a two-day trip there, I was able to find a home in Santee that had gone into foreclosure at a very reasonable price. Little did I know that this purchase price would be considered among the lowest in the San Diego market for many years to come. The very next month, the market started to soar again, making it very difficult for many to purchase. God knew the future and that that financial investment would actually serve me in other interesting ways in the days to come.

In June 2012, I boarded a plane for a three-week exploration trip to Zambia. I was hoping to more clearly define my role in the country I had been directed to for more than six months. Soon after arriving, I found myself asking my taxi driver to "chase an ambulance." Zambia does not have a coordinated EMS system like we appreciate in the United States. Seeing an ambulance drop off a patient at the hospital left me curious. Who were these ambulance workers, and what type of training did they have? After arriving where the ambulance workers trained, I was impressed by this volunteer organization that was attempting to provide services to trauma victims and also patients needing hospital transfers. I provided some classes to help them gain some additional skills during the subsequent few weeks.

On that first visit, I also thoroughly enjoyed my time at Mother Theresa's orphanage, where I was able to hold babies and teach preschool children how to do the hokey-pokey. They were thrilled with their coloring books and animal-shaped balloons. I felt right at home in this radically different culture that somehow felt like the United States when I was growing up. Change was happening but not at the technological speed of the United States. Zambians were not born with cell phones at their fingertips, and Internet was still quite unreliable. I heard that in the villages some climbed mango trees for better reception!

Relationships and faith were priorities to the Zambian people. It was one of the few nations declared to be Christian, with more than 95 percent of the population followers of Christianity. They respected their elders, seeking their wisdom and valuing their gray hair. The introduction of antiviral therapy was beneficial, but with more than 17 percent of the Lusaka population having been tested positive for HIV according to the World Health Organization, life expectancy in the country was just reaching the average of fifty years. As I prayed for clarity on how I could help this overwhelmingly needy country, the dean of the primary medical school in the country, the University of Zambia (UNZA), asked for a meeting with me. Dean Goma showed me an empty room and told me that the equipment for a clinical-skills lab had been ordered, but they had no one to teach. He wanted me to consider a full-time position. This was exactly what I had been doing for the past three years! The Lord does prepare us for the next steps on our journeys because He alone knows our future.

Despite the circumstantial evidence that there was a need and a position I could fill, I wanted to hear from the Lord. Was this where He would have me serve? I told the dean I would pray and let him know before I flew home in a few days. The next day, June 24, 2012, I attended church, fully expecting the Lord to confirm His will by the end of the day. That morning during worship, one song struck at my heart. It was a song I would only hear once in all the years I would spend in Africa: "Here I Am, Lord" by James Kilbane.

I, the Lord of sea and sky,
I have heard My people cry.
All who dwell in dark and sin,
My hand will save.
I who made the stars of night,
I will make their darkness bright.
Who will bear My light to them?
Whom shall I send?

The sermon from the pastor followed, using Jeremiah 8: 21–22: "Since my people are crushed, I am crushed: I mourn, and horror grips me. Is there no balm in Gilead? Is there no physician there? Why then is there no healing for the wound of my people?"

There are only a few verses in the Bible that use the term "physician." Those verses captured my attention. I also had a good sense of why some of the people were not healed and so many were dying in Africa. There was a great shortage of experienced physicians available to teach; most were involved in direct patient care. Medical schools were increasing the number of students to meet the country's need, but those students needed someone to teach them how to do excellent physical exams and to process the data to properly diagnose and treat.

This was the second of the two confirming "verily, verily" experiences I needed: the song and the words preached. God wanted me in Africa full-time and gave me a clear vision of what I would be doing. It was time to return home, sell what I had, and say good-byes to my friends and family. It was bittersweet saying good-bye, uncertain when I would see them again, yet I had clarity on the call to go.

On December 12, 2012, I was heading to Zambia, and within a few weeks, I began teaching my first class. This short writing reflects some of my earliest thoughts and feelings during those first few weeks.

January 12, 2013

The Land of Opportunities

The halls are poorly lit and musty. The bathroom sinks have tasted soap and water years ago, and there are no signs that paper towels were ever an option. The pale paint in the halls has been lost years ago as students passed by with dreams to change the world. The limping brown wooden chairs reflect the economic history, and no electronics grace the shared desks. Learning to be a physician in Zambia looks different from what I have known in the "land of opportunities."

The first day of launching the new clinical skills class begins with a rumble of expectations. Deep in the soil of the soul of each medical student lies a dream that I unearth with the question, "If you could do anything, what would it be?"

> The answers are as varied as the hues of a rainbow. The flight to the moon, finding the cure for AIDS, or playing on the national soccer team bear resemblance to dreams I have heard on the other side of this world. One response, however, strikes at the heart of the unspoken pain of these ninety-six young men and women: "Buy chemotherapy for cancer patients and employ some workers to take care of those neglected right in the hospital."
>
> The challenges of a poverty-stricken country can, at times, ground those who desire to soar with their dreams. Looking beyond the harsh reality of this medical system, I find a glimmer of hope that my dream to encourage compassionate and excellent physicians will be successful. A tear drops as I read the final response. "If I could do anything at all today, I would hang out with orphans or the poor and just make them feel loved."

I have been welcomed to another land of opportunities.

This opportunity would be my greatest academic challenge. The students in this pilot group would be given only six weeks, a few hours each week, to learn what I prioritized. In the United States, the curriculum was spread out over two years, giving students plenty of time to practice and memorize. After this initial group, I would assess the results and revise the curriculum for a full-year program. What I had not fully appreciated was that I would have ninety-six students to teach hands-on clinical skills and no assistants. Learning how to do neurological exams, including deep tendon reflexes, how to hold the hammer and strike the knee just right to get a response, would take time and need multiple trainers. Back in the United States, I had a ratio of one experienced trainer to seven students. Obviously, this was not the United States. I murmured, "But, Lord, what will I do?"

Fortunately, a few more senior students arrived at the lab one day to offer their services. They were curious about what this American doctor was offering in the new course. Since they were busy with their own medical school obligations, I had limited time to train them in a whole new approach to the physical exam, but I would give them some direction the night before a lab session, and they would do their best the next day. I was also able to recruit a few other foreign physicians to assist me at times with lectures or labs. "See one, do one, teach one," a familiar motto in medicine, played out over and over. It was challenging for all of us. Our motto was: "Flexibility is our best ability." Though not an ideal situation, it did open my eyes to the potential of utilizing the senior students more fully if they were given a more comprehensive training program.

During the long school break in July 2013, that opportunity came, and I recruited additional fifth-, sixth-, and seventh-year students and trained them, and together, we trained a smaller group of thirty fourth-year students who had not attended the initial pilot program earlier in the year. "Training the trainers who would train trainers" was my new mantra.

First graduates of the academic assistants' training program (senior peer educators), August 2013.

By the fall of 2013, I was ready to do a full-year course with a group of trained trainers to assist me with the lab sessions. They had some understanding of learning theory and were reliable in grading and in the methods of giving feedback that could encourage their younger colleagues. We continued to add curriculum throughout the year as I discovered more areas of need. I wanted to prepare the students for the intensity of the clinical settings that they would encounter after completing my program.

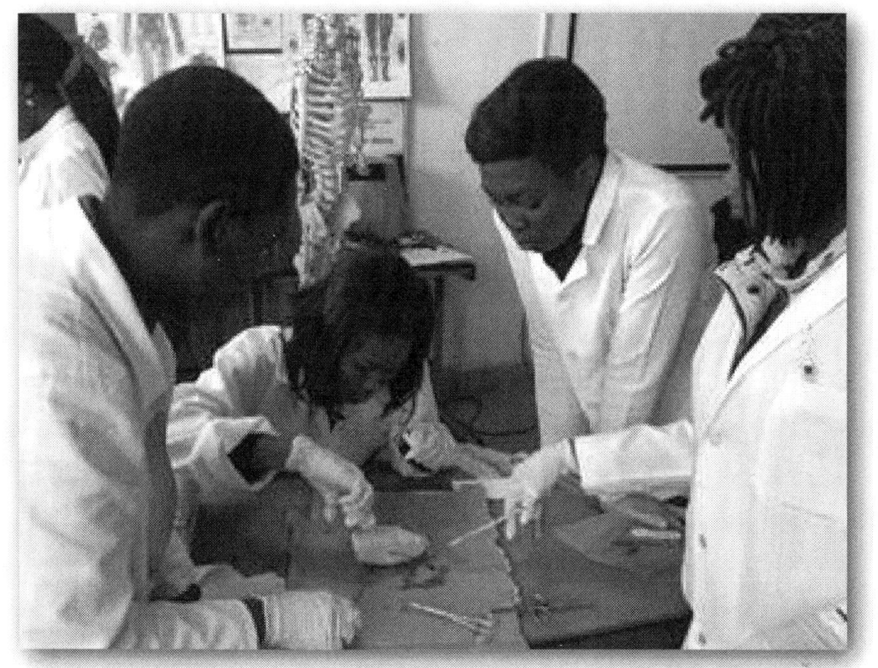

Academic assistants teaching their junior peers how to suture.

In keeping with the theme of training trainers, I helped coordinate five United States–based volunteer teams in response to requests from the clinical and academic faculty. Working alongside my colleagues in various practical workshops was very rewarding, and I was grateful for the assistance of the Christian Medical and Dental Association, specifically Medical Education International (MEI), in helping with the recruitment of these teams with expertise in faculty development, psychiatry, and emergency/disaster response.

Physicians with Medical Education International (Christian Medical and Dental Association) training emergency physicians and surgeons in Zambia.

The university hospital patients were the most ill people the country had to offer, often arriving very late because of delays in transport or referrals from the smaller outlying clinics or hospitals. It was clear that the number of patients arriving in the emergency department daily would overwhelm the trained resources. Even on the medical and surgical floors, every day was like a disaster day when there were limited trained personnel, medications, and other supplies. Triage skills were required. This was where my emergency medicine background really paid off.

With the assistance of some teams arriving from the United States, I was able to train students how to triage (sort patients based on their risk of death). Their practical final testing occurred during a mock disaster like those I had staged during the international Partners for Life programs. We used makeup, chicken bones, and ketchup, and yes, it was just like a Hollywood movie with lots of blood and guts. I trained people to act as if they were genuinely injured or in pain. It was dramatic, and certainly some of the "patients" died unnecessarily as the doctors in training were trying to apply their academic lessons to the "real-life" scenarios in front of them. There were great lessons and much laughter throughout the event, and it became a favorite addition to the curriculum at the end of each year.

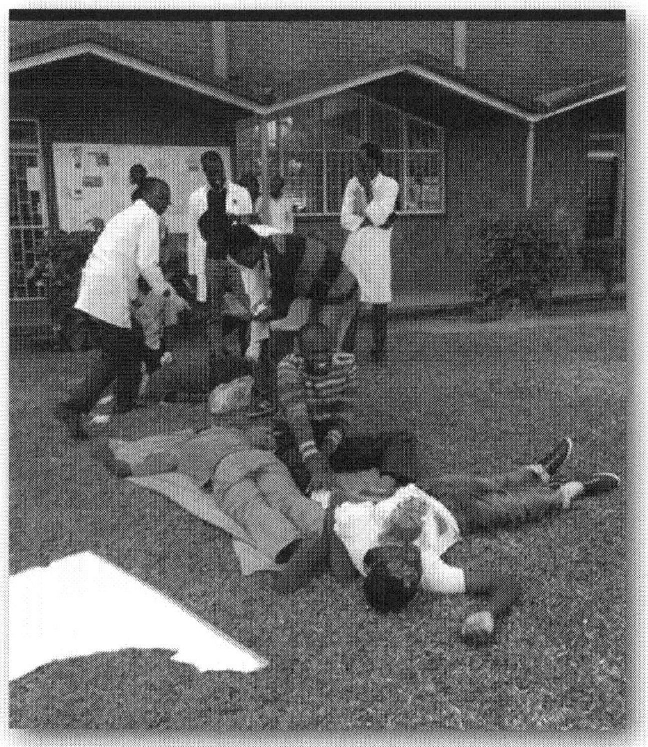

Disaster training for student doctors.

While developing the academic assistants program to help train medical students, I developed wonderful relationships with these students I was mentoring to be teachers. We would have pizza and movie nights, soccer days, and lots of laughter. They taught me so much about their culture and helped me feel I was surrounded by family. Whenever I had a need, I knew I could call on them to help me to figure out what to do. They were so resourceful!

Through these relationship-building times, I also found there were significant spiritual needs in the patients at the hospital as well as in the medical students themselves. A few of the more advanced students I had never met had committed suicide the previous year, fatalities that could be attributed to the disillusionment that had resulted from the horrendous workload in such a resource-limited country. They were in unrecognized spiritual crisis, and the contributions they could have made to their people were forever lost. I offered to be available to students with spiritual needs, and often students would come to me in tears over a stressful life event. After some time spent talking, we often concluded our sessions with times of prayer, which would bring hope. The hospital had a few retired chaplains to cover more than two thousand patients, plus all their family members and staff. Caring for the needs of medical students wasn't feasible. The problem was huge, and I knew I needed to do something more. It was during a hospital training program that a solution was conceived.

During the break from school, I offered my assistance in training the staff at a hospital in Lusaka. I coordinated a holistic training program and recruited a team of nurses and EMS workers to assist me. We incorporated spiritual-health assessment into the program in the same way I had done with the Partners for Life teams in Turkey, Mongolia, and China, and a few local pastors assisted with that component of the training. Those pastors were so rewarded by the impact this had on the staff they asked me to help them develop a college to train more pastors to be chaplains and especially to have the skills to intervene with suicidal patients or parishioners.

During my career in the emergency department, I had assisted many patients who had attempted suicide. I knew there were great needs for specialized training for this worldwide, and yet there were very few resources in Zambia. There were only three psychiatrists in a country of fifteen million people, and I had heard of only one psychologist. In fact, if someone tried to commit suicide and survived, he or she was sometimes beaten to death by police or neighbors who believed he or she was possessed by a demon of suicide. Mental illness was not well understood and was often grouped into the category of demon possession. People took family members to pastors, not psychiatrists, for intervention. Training and educating pastors about mental health, psychosocial counseling, medical terminology, and culturally appropriate interventions could be very beneficial to all.

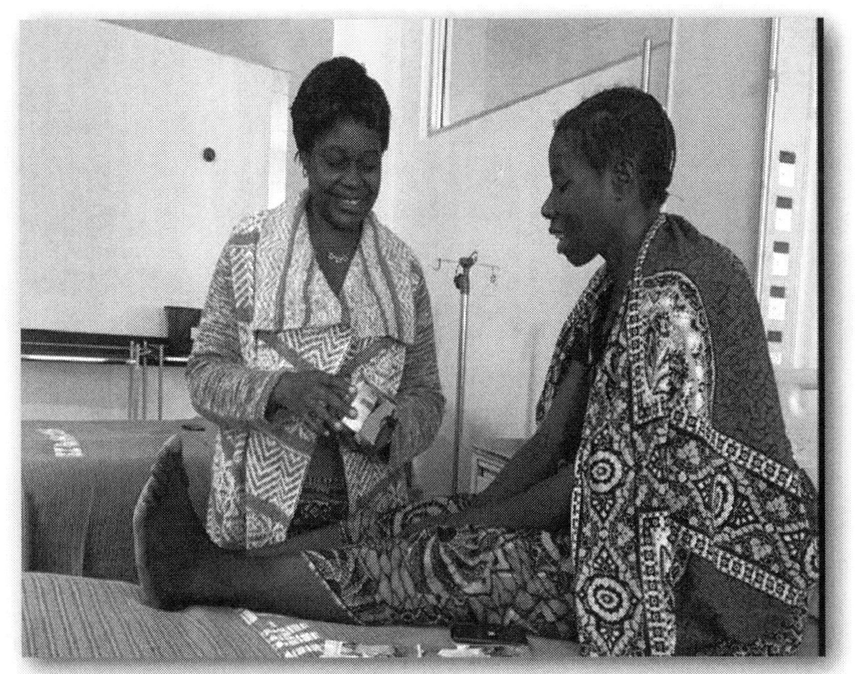

Trinity Chaplain College chaplain Josephine talking with a cancer patient.

Trinity Chaplain College began with a small group of Zambian pastors with big hearts for their country. *Trinity* was to represent the Father, the Son, and the Holy Spirit and also the triune nature of man: spiritual, emotional, and physical. The college was interdenominational, sharing a common faith statement, and began to meet at Beit CURE Hospital, a ministry focused on the congenital anomalies of children. These children were considered cursed in this culture, which often left their mothers isolated and unsupported. The hospital had a nurturing Christian setting to begin training future chaplains to do the work of ministry among this very needy group of children and their parents. Chaplain and psychological training teams from the United States came at various times to teach, providing the foundation of the training program. In time, graduates of the program assisted with the training of subsequent classes.

First graduating class of Trinity Chaplain College, November 2014.

The two groups often worked together, medical students examining the chaplain students and the chaplain students helping the medical students understand spiritual-health assessment. The pastors loved role-playing as patients and learning more about their own anatomy and physiology and how various medical conditions could manifest. Social issues such as domestic violence were given a voice through role-play to help these future doctors ask the right questions and do proper assessments. I found curriculum development and teaching medical perspective on areas that were culturally challenging, such as seizures, mental health disorders, and congenital defects, to be very stimulating. I learned a lot from my pastor students.

One of the most important integrations of the two groups occurred with "Telling Bad News." I had introduced this course at the medical school in Washington, and it was appreciated there, but it was needed even more in this African culture, where HIV affected so many and cancer was rampant due to poor nutrition and lack of vaccines.

Through the introduction of spiritual and mental health curricula, medical students learned the benefits of a holistic medical approach. Often in evaluations, they said that those components were the most interesting to them. These responses seemed to be in such contrast to what I had experienced in the US medical school. I thrived in this secular medical school environment where I had total freedom to discuss spirituality.

Challenges in communication and time persisted throughout my tenure in Zambia. Just when I thought I had adjusted to the many British terms used for common items, I would be surprised. One day a man approached me while I was having my car filled with gas. He asked if everything was OK under my bonnet. Not having put on any sort of hat that day, I was perplexed. He repeated the words a little louder as if that would help. On his third attempt, he motioned to the hood, and then it all made sense. Full-service gas stations where fluid levels could be checked were a vague memory for me.

Meeting times would always be a source of difficulty for me. You can put a type A personality in Africa, but you cannot take the type A personality out. When a meeting was set for 8:00 a.m., many would wander in about 10:00 a.m. without any excuse, but I would be quite alone at the earlier hour. By giving stern threats of serious damage to grades, I could get most of my medical students to comply, but without any ramifications in other settings, I was the one that needed to adjust—not the nation of Zambia.

Of course, during the years I spent in Africa, I missed family and friends, but using Skype when the Internet was working allowed me to have nearly weekly conversations. I also was blessed by a visit from my younger daughter in November 2014. She was a part of the World Race, a traveling group of forty young people doing short-term missions in a variety of countries for eleven months. I was able to host many of them for a traditional Thanksgiving meal. The temperatures in Zambia in November are often in the nineties, so we grilled the turkey outside, but we were able to find all the fixings, and this group was encouraged by the taste of home on a significant American holiday.

During the final month of my tenure in Zambia, my older daughter was able to join me for some sightseeing through a few surrounding African countries. Being a tourist in some of the remote settings we found ourselves in, it was educational and very interesting. We listened how the herbalists in Botswana would dig up roots for various ailments and bury a water-filled ostrich egg in the sub-Saharan desert, which could be found during times of long journeys. The polers also trained us in their trade of balancing our weight while standing in rocking canoes as we tried to paddle forward toward our destination. Needless to say, there were a few unexpected splashes. The herbalists in Namibia shared how they would select the next generation of herbalists to train based on whether or not they were born in the amniotic sac. This would be a divine sign of the chosen one. Besides our wonderful experiences with the country people in many settings, we enjoyed seeing African animals in their native habitats.

Below is a reflection on one of those experiences on a safari in South Luangwa National Park:

Dancing with the Elephant

Turbulence tossed us back and forth in the final descent to the tarmac runway. The African sun was high in the sky, and the "international" airport at Mfuwe was anything but cosmopolitan. The local dark-skinned men worked hard to transfer the few bags to the terminal, and we collected our belongings and headed to camp. The murky waters of the Luangwa River boasted the most hippos in the world. Their bulging eyes peeked up over small ripples, and their rock-shaped bodies glistened in the hot orange sun. Black-faced monkeys swung from low branches, chattering as they went. Old dried vines draped some of the trees, reminding me of the scenery from the movie *Tarzan*.

We had been warned after arrival to our camp about dangers of the roaming hippos and gray elephants in the early evening hours. They had their rights to cross the river and climb the banks to invade the human camp at will. We would need to oblige them but not feed them. All snacks must be removed from our bags and stored in refrigerated glass bins to minimize the chances of being sniffed out by the large mammals. We would need to travel from our tents at night with the watchmen who would carry "torches" and protect us from the parade of nocturnal wildlife including the leopards, lions, and hyenas.

On cue, as the afternoon sun began to set in the sky, the elephants began crossing the Luangwa River, single file past the mummified crocodiles that sunned themselves along the banks. We were mesmerized watching them forging into our camp, grabbing high and low branches with a stranglehold. Methodically, they were pulling off the bright green leaves, rolling them into a pile on their gray snout, and shoveling them into their mouth. My five-feet-three-inch frame seemed to shrink as I gazed at the one-story-size moving pachyderm. I considered the branching nearby sausage tree as a possible escape route should my stilled presence intersect with the desired pathway.

As the shadows of the acacia trees increased on the landscape and the sky turned a variety of pastel colors heralding the setting sun, I ventured back to my tent. Freshly armed with long-sleeved clothing to fend off the anticipated onslaught of malaria-transferring mosquitoes, I quickly zipped up the tent to prevent the entrance of unwanted flying or crawling insects. Stepping a few feet from the tent, I was suddenly stopped in my tracks. Hovering less than eight feet from me was a fifteen-foot-tall elephant, just as startled as I was, and together we synchronized our swing steps backward and out of view of one another.

"Stand still, don't move!" came the forceful warning from the camp owner who had previously spoken of the dangers of the elephants and had just watched the elephant become startled by some mysterious figure on the other side of the tent.

Frozen in place, I strained my ears to listen for the rustle of broken leaves or branches, hoping the elephant would choose a quiet retreat rather than a charge. Only silence. How much time had passed as I waited for his move? Has it been one minute…five minutes, less or more? Finally inching myself toward the corner of the camouflaged green tent, I peeked around…

Nothing. No sign of an elephant, footprint, or even a broken branch. Stealthily as he had appeared, he must have retreated and found himself safely back at home in the crocodile-infested waters of the Luangwa River. I was left only with a memory of a very special dance with an elephant.

In February 2015, after more than two years in country, I was sensing that both programs were well enough developed to be continued with national trainers directing them. I had drafted a research paper on the work with the academic assistants, which would be published later with the intent of helping others who had similar desires to join nationals in establishing clinical-skills programs.[1] As a result of that experience, I appreciated a new vision of continuing to train trainers who would train trainers to train trainers. My prayers focused on clarity and further direction on location. I considered a return to the United States and sent out a few resumes.

In April, I was on a Skype conversation with the president of San Diego Christian College about a position in its science department. He was surprised to find that I had a condo in Santee, the same community in which the school was located and where he wanted his professors to live. Amazingly, before even leaving for Zambia, the Lord had provided the necessary direction to the right home in the town where my future employment would be—even before the school was opened at that location. I was returning home to the United States of America!

Lord, thank You for Your guidance that takes us to places we can only imagine but prepares us for those places even before we set foot on the soil.
Amen.

Notes

1. Cheryl Snyder and Rose Chisenga, "Impact of a Pre-clinical Skills Course with Peer Assisted Learning (PAL) on Preparedness and Confidence Levels of Medical Students in Africa," *Christian Journal for Global Health* 4, no. 1 (March 2017): 3–12.

CHAPTER 10

Return

RED, WHITE, AND BLUE FLAGS waving in the breeze were a welcoming sight as I arrived back in the United States. Though I had thoroughly enjoyed my time in Africa, seeing family and friends again was like a drink of cold water on a hot summer day. I was also looking forward to beginning a new role as a professor at San Diego Christian College, where I would be teaching anatomy and physiology, biology, health education, and nutrition to the next generation of doctors, nurses, and paraprofessionals.

My mission was clear: training trainers to train trainers who will train trainers. Weaving in stories of my travels in Africa and previous medical encounters (without patient names, of course) helped keep the students engaged. I found this competitive world of electronics extremely challenging as a professor. In Africa, cell phones were present in class but not Wi-Fi, so competing with students on their phones was less common. As in every country, regardless of distractions, there are always those students who inspire their teachers through their own commitment to academics. I have fond memories of students with such commitment in each of my classes.

What was most rewarding was identifying students who shared my passion to bring their knowledge to Africa and to learn from the African people. One graduating psychology student, Kelsie, felt the Lord was giving her clear direction to join me on my return visit in May 2016. We talked about the needs in the area of psychology; she had heard of the high rates of alcohol abuse and suicide. Some statistics showed that as many as one in five adults in Zambia were abusing alcohol, and some started even as children. When it became cold and/or they found themselves hungry, there were local "home brews" available on their streets that would help ease their discomfort. Often, by the time they reached their twenties, alcohol was already a part of their lifestyle. They clung to it, depending on it to survive the daily harsh reality of poverty. This unfortunate pattern, in turn, contributed to job loss, health issues, domestic violence, and even more poverty.

Kelsie suggested introducing the international program Celebrate Recovery to the Zambian psychologists and psychiatrists, and we gathered some necessary curriculum supplies. While in Africa, we introduced the program to a group of psychologists and psychiatrists, and it was well received. A few chaplains and medical students also wanted to learn more about this possible solution to such a well-known social problem. The Alcoholics Anonymous (AA) program had been introduced years before, but it had not been well accepted by the people because the program encouraged people to rely on a higher power rather than specifically Jesus Christ. The mental health professionals believed a biblical-based program would be better accepted. Celebrate Recovery also focused on addressing the root cause of the drinking, more specifically the individual's "hurts, habits, or other hang-ups." This, of course, could be beneficial for a greater diversity of emotional pain or behaviors that were not resulting in healthy lifestyles.

Benjamin Samusiko was chosen as the program leader because of his years of experience in leading the AA program and his passion to have a more comprehensive and effective program. Kelsie and I returned to the United States with newfound passion and clarity about our role. We helped in raising funds to assist Benjamin with travel expenses, and he arrived in the United States in August 2016 to attend the Celebrate Recovery's national leaders' conference hosted by the founding church, Saddleback Community Church, located only a few hours from my home. Celebrate Recovery (CR) had been providing training to church leaders for more than twenty-five years and at that time was located in more than thirty thousand churches in 125 countries. Zambia would be a new frontier. Besides attending the conference, he visited many Celebrate Recovery groups in southern California and presented the needs in Zambia. Journey Community Church in San Diego was most receptive to the need and began to mobilize a team of its most experienced leaders to join us on a return trip to Zambia, where they could train church leaders in the CR principles.

A year later, in May 2017, we had the opportunity to return with the largest team I had ever mobilized. There were sixteen total team members, seven of us from San Diego Christian College, including a psychology professor. We had three separate teams: medical, psychological, and Celebrate Recovery. On It was very rewarding to see the first Celebrate Recovery program for Zambia launched in a church in Lusaka on May 25, 2017. One of the attendees was a man addicted to heroin, who had been referred by the psychology team. He was deeply moved on hearing the testimonies of our Celebrate Recovery team members, and hope was on the horizon for him, as well as many other Zambians with hurts, habits, and hang-ups.

Though we met all together at times, we also separated into smaller groups, where we were able to focus on specific areas of teaching. The psychological team was able to assist in training medical students, psychiatrists, psychologists in training, and house moms in an orphanage. They also offered counseling sessions for the medical students to help identify those who might have been suffering from severe depression or other mental health disorders. The medical team not only focused on the medical students but also did very practical lectures and labs for emergency physicians and surgeons. The college students were inspired to return as they were mentored by an experienced leader in their major area of study and also had prepared lectures to share with our African friends. Truly, it was a fulfillment of the motto "Training trainers to train trainers who would train trainers."

During our visit, the medical team provided an intense two-week training focused on various emergencies and lifesaving skills. The academic assistants I had previously trained had already prepared their more junior medical students through training in physical exams and other procedures. Our team of emergency physicians helped provide additional training in preparation of our mock disaster training. Once again, it was a huge success, and through the intense training, the largest class ever of 160 medical students graduated. The class president gratefully expressed how the students had now fully grasped the value of providing holistic care to patients and, specifically, the importance of developing their own spirituality to sustain them through the difficulties they would face in the years to come.

Return to Zambia with the US team, May 2017.
Training trainers at UNZA Medical School.

My second return to Zambia was clearly successful, and after the amazing training team for the United States, I flew alone to Ethiopia. This was a new country for me, and I had been directed to make a visit after prayer and multiple encounters with people during the month of April prior to departing for Zambia. I learned the Korean church had built the medical school and Myungsung Medical Center (MMC) in Addis Ababa, partnering with Samaritan's Purse, which assisted with the recruitment and processing of physicians. Specifically, there was a need for science professors and physicians to help with the training of medical students from their early years through their clinical experience. My years of experience as an emergency physician and, most recently, as a professor of sciences during the previous two years prepared me for their need.

The setting was very multiethnic, with American, Korean, and Ethiopian colleagues working alongside one another for God's glory and the needs of the people of Ethiopia. We ate Korean kimchee for breakfast, lunch, and dinner, along with a few exotically seasoned Ethiopian menu items with injera (their flat bread). Occasionally, there were American options, such as pancakes, and always plenty of fresh garden vegetables. I felt right at home working alongside Dr. David Jester, a visiting emergency physician, giving ten lectures and making patient rounds. Many patients had burns as a result of cooking on open fires. One child had been mauled by a hyena while she slept outside her hut with her mother. The courageous battle had ensued between the child's mother and the hyena, resulting in the mother pulling the child out of the beast's fangs. She survived, but not without significant facial damage that the very talented surgical team would find challenging. This certainly was a new cause of injury for a Western-trained physician!

During my short stay, I was also able to present my testimony during four chapels, one for physicians and staff; one for patients, staff, and families; and the remaining two for the medical students. Reflecting on what the Lord had done during my time with cancer and his faithfulness in giving me health for the past nine years was encouraging for all of us. During my visit, I was also able to join in a meeting with hospital leaders from the city, including United Nations and US embassy representatives. Discussions at that meeting revealed a high level of interest in developing the emergency medical system (EMS) program as a full service to expedite care and transfers. There was interest in incorporating MMC, so together we drafted a proposal to strategize the development at Myungsung, and the hospital CEO was very favorable toward the concepts presented. I left Ethiopia, very hopeful that I would be able to use my various skills and experience in the days to come.

My return to the United States came with not only joyful reflection but also a surprise. On my flight home, at an altitude somewhere around thirty-six thousand feet on the more than twenty-hour flight back to Seattle, I developed a cough. Despite a few weeks of rest while visiting in the Pacific Northwest, the cough did not abate. After returning to San Diego, I went for my morning swim, as I had many times before, but realized I could not even swim one lap without feeling like I was suffocating. What was wrong?

I pulled out my stethoscope and listened to my lungs. Left side normal, right side varying from very diminished to absent breath sounds in the right upper, middle, and lower lobes! Self-diagnosis led to my assumption that I had contracted an atypical pneumonia. Early on the following Monday morning, I went to an urgent care clinic and had an x-ray taken. Unsuspecting, I had entered the slippery slope of changing roles once again.

The chest x-ray showed a large right pleural effusion, fluid in between the two linings of my lung. In my experience as a physician, there were other possible diagnoses with a similar x-ray, but with my cancer history, metastasis was the most likely culprit. I checked into the local emergency department and waited beneath a cold white sheet on a gurney. After the removal of a liter of old bloody fluid, hope, too, was drained. The last drop of hope of a different diagnosis vanished before the ink was dry on the final pathology report. Cancer was demanding my full attention once again. Those rebellious cells that had stealthily defied death by toxic chemicals, surgery, and radiation more than nine years before had grown in number. Not a true return since they had never left, but once again, I sensed they had commandeered my plans.

I left the ED anticipating improved stamina on a reflective local-beach hike. Unfortunately, despite the large volume of fluid removed, I felt very little difference in my shortness of breath. The next day, I moved forward with coordination of care and tried to schedule with my previous oncologist, but he wanted the final pathology report before booking the appointment. Knowing I would still need the chest fluid drained, I scheduled an appointment with a pulmonologist. Those plans would be obliterated when, within the next forty-eight hours, increasing chest pain and shortness of breath would force me to return to the ED.

After removing about one and a half liters of fluid on the second visit, and with a confirmed diagnosis of metastatic breast cancer, the doctors strongly recommended I stay overnight to speed up the process for my insurance company to qualify me for oncology services. During the next two weeks, there were almost daily visits to doctors or specialized imaging exams, placement of a chest tube so I could drain the pleural fluid at home daily, and the start of oral chemo drugs. After the initial testing, I felt prompting by the Holy Spirit, so I encouraged my physician to order an MRI on my brain. She complied reluctantly as it was outside protocol and I did not manifest any neurological changes. She was quite surprised to find a brain tumor. I, too, was surprised and alarmed to know the cancer had progressed to my brain, the last frontier of tissue we associate with our intellect and will. I was grateful that, within a week, the radiation oncologist and neurosurgeon teamed up for rapid eradication of the intruder.

Oddly enough, the unwanted "gift" of cancer was still wrapped in choice. I could choose to be overcome with fear and anxiety or fully surrender every cell in my body to the care of the Great Physician. He alone knew my future and the course of my days on earth. The final summary of a multitude of scans revealed that the cancer had reached its tentacles into the chest, bone, and brain besides the pleural effusion. The prognosis was medically dismal, but spiritually, I was still aware that I walked with the God of miracles. I would trust Him for strength day by day and believe I would not leave this earth a second too early. I chose to trust Him through this return visit to the valley of the shadow of death. I had passed through one in the past, and He had been faithful to walk with me each step of the way. I was persuaded that this journey as well would be for my good and His glory. Experience and gratitude for the years I had been granted already left me with a peace as I looked into the dark future. Though illness is not a part of His perfect plan and will not be a part of His perfect heavenly kingdom, He is able to use the events of this fallen world to help us reach out to the lost and hurting souls all around us.

> And we know that for those who love God all things work together for good, for those who are called according to his purpose. (Rom. 8:28, ESV)

The most painful part of this second valley experience once again was telling my family. Nearly a decade had passed since I had declared the cancer news to my family. I had taught the subject of "Telling Bad News" on many occasions and in many countries. It did not make it any easier. My older daughter had just got married earlier that month. My younger daughter was expecting her first baby (and my first grandbaby!) in just about three months. My mom was now eighty-five years old and had had family deaths to grieve earlier in the year. There never is a good time to tell bad news, and I delayed as long as I possibly could, but ultimately, I wished I could have at least been there in person instead of telling them by phone.

Besides my family, I shared the news with my friends and former students throughout the world. As the news of the return of my cancer spread, so did the outpouring of prayers and support. Now with the advent of smartphones and Wi-Fi, WhatsApp, and other methods of international communication at my fingertips, I had daily doses of encouragement. Countless times when the gravity of my situation took its toll on my faith, a message would come to buoy me up to hope again, and I would find strength to carry on.

After diagnosis, the initiation of oral chemotherapy unfortunately saw only progression of the cancer, as seen in the blood tumor markers and additional scans. I was forced to accept that the latest and greatest FDA-approved specialty drug designed to target breast cancer was ineffective, and I started on a different oral chemotherapy. I prioritized visiting friends and family in the Pacific Northwest. On one vibrant October weekend as the leaves were changing to their majestic colors, I was able to encourage a group of ministry leaders at a Be Still retreat in Washington. These retreats for women, in which I had participated during the past, are a tremendous source of spiritual strength. The theme of the retreat this year was designated far in advance—"It Is Well with My Soul"—in keeping with the hymn by Horatio Spafford quoted earlier. After that time of spiritual refreshment, I was able to greet my beautiful granddaughter, Jasmine Rae, who was only a few hours old.

The visit was short, and the increasing chest pain and tumor markers prompted me to consider other treatment options. Four previous intravenous chemo drugs and two different oral agents were unable to halt the cancer progression. Time was running out, and I was looking to the Great Physician to direct my next steps of medical care.

Through the years since my initial diagnosis in 2008, I have researched various international approaches to cancer care. There were many options in various other countries that seemed to demonstrate positive results but that, unfortunately, had not been approved by the US Food and Drug

Administration. Currently in the United States, there is a specialty field of medicine known as integrative or functional medicine. Integrative medicine is an approach to care that puts the patient at the center and addresses the full range of physical, emotional, mental, social, spiritual, and environmental influences that affect a person's health. Employing a personalized strategy that considers the patient's unique conditions, needs, and circumstances, it uses the most appropriate interventions from an array of scientific disciplines to heal illness and disease and help people regain and maintain optimum health.[1]

Besides traditional options, these specialists also incorporate alternative or complementary approaches for a holistic treatment plan. The American College for Advancement in Medicine[2] is an excellent source of information. It is possible to become a board-certified specialist, and they have their own peer-reviewed, evidence-based journal as well. The Academy of Integrative Health & Medicine (AIHM) is an interprofessional association of integrative clinicians offering a fellowship and conferences throughout the nation to keep updated.[3] Two of my doctors in the United States had recommended that I consider the option of treatment in Mexico, since it was so close to San Diego, and they knew of effective, therapeutic options that were not available in the United States. They had seen some promising results in patients who had sought care specifically at the Hope 4 Cancer Clinic's Tijuana location.[4] I agreed I needed to consider options that would boost my immune system and not inhibit my fighter cells from detecting the cancer like all previously prescribed chemo drugs had done.

I started a twenty-one-day program on site. The treatments included intravenous treatments with immune-boosting drugs, ultrasonic and photo therapies, ultraviolet blood irradiation, detoxifying and hyperthermia, hyperbaric oxygen chamber treatments, and highly nutritious food and supplements. I drank alkalized water to help alter the pH in my blood slightly, making it less of a friendly environment for the cancer cells. I also met people from all over the world who were seeking assistance with their cancer care. People of a wide range of ages: one only in high school and others with white hair in their seventies. Most, of course, were from the United States or Canada, but some were from Australia, New Zealand, China, Africa, and the Dominican Republic. We were a diverse group in some ways, but we shared the common threat of cancer. We were encouraged by one another's company during our meals and at the evening worship services. Furthermore, we learned about various treatment options from one another and why some of them worked better than others. Patients returning for their three-month checkups shared good reports, which encouraged the rest of us.

At the conclusion of the program, my tumor markers as measured before and after by my US physician had dropped by 40–50 percent! No chemotherapy could attest to those dramatic changes. I was quite hopeful. I proceeded with a chest surgery to allow me to be free of drainage tubes and began regaining strength daily. On December 1, 2017, I was able to swim again, which was a real joy after being restricted to showers only for more than four months. But a few days later, riding on the infamous cancer roller coaster, I discovered the tumor markers had increased threefold in the past month, indicating significant tumor progression. Oral chemotherapy that I had stopped prior to surgery was resumed to try to slow down the progression. December is a great month to wait for miracles as the world reflects on the miracle of the Creator of the universe entering the womb of a virgin so He could be birthed into our world, clothed in humanity. His sacrifice as our Savior Jesus alone opens the doors to eternity in heaven, where the roller coaster of life on earth ends and His endless praises begin.

As I close this final chapter in my life story, I am convinced of the hope I have and know that my story is not over. It will continue to live out through the lives I have been blessed to know. Should the Lord choose to provide me additional time and stamina, I will return to Ethiopia to share some of my previous experiences and knowledge with the hope that it can assist the medical students. Dr. Jeff Thompson, one of the doctors on the Zambia team in May 2017 (standing behind me in the group picture), has safely arrived in Ethiopia to begin his one-year commitment to the work of developing a stronger emergency medical response in the country. He will continue to coordinate efforts and training teams for the days to come.

"Faith is determining to trust God when He has not answered all the questions or even assured a pain-free passage."[5] I am persuaded that my ultimate healing will occur on my final move to my true home in heaven, where there will be no more sorrow or suffering. I am at peace knowing the Great Physician who loves me will call me home when my work is done on earth. Right on time.

If you would like to track my updates, please visit my blog at Changing Places https://plus.google.com/collection/AovQXE.If you have any personal comments or questions, please feel free to e-mail me at changingplaces2018@gmail.com.

Bless you in your journey of knowing and loving Him better every day!

Cheryl

Dr. Snyder at Victoria Falls, Zambia

Thank you, Lord, for the opportunity to share the journey You chose for me. May it bring You glory, and may it result in more around the throne of God giving You praise!

Amen.

After this I looked, and there before me was a great multitude that no one could count, from every nation, tribe, people and language, standing before the throne and before the Lamb. They were wearing white robes and were holding palm branches in their hands. And they cried out in a loud voice: "Salvation belongs to our God, who sits on the throne, and to the Lamb."

> All the angels were standing around the throne and around the elders and the four living creatures. They fell down on their faces before the throne and worshiped God, saying: "Amen! Praise and glory and wisdom and thanks and honor and power and strength be to our God for ever and ever. Amen!"
>
> (Rev. 7:9–12, NIV)

> Let this be recorded for future generations, so that a people not yet born will praise the Lord. Tell them the Lord looked down from his heavenly sanctuary. He looked down to earth from heaven to hear the groans of the prisoners, to release those condemned to die. And so the Lord's fame will be celebrated in Zion, his praises in Jerusalem, when multitudes gather together and kingdoms come to worship the Lord.
>
> (Ps. 102:18–22, NLT)

Notes

1. https://www.dukeintegrativemedicine.org/about/what-is-integrative-medicine/
2. ACAM: American College for Advancement in Medicine http://www.acam.org/?
3. https://www.aihm.org/page/fellowship.
4. https://hope4cancer.com.
5. J. C. Dobson, In the Arms of God (Wheaton, IL: Tyndale House Publishers Inc., 1997). Part 7 page 3.

ADDENDUM
BINOCULAR VISION OF AFRICA

Short writings from my first six months in Zambia, December 2012–May 2013:

December 26, 2012: TIA (This is Africa)

From the dark pigmented skin to the brightness of the equatorial sun, it is a land of contrasts and surprises.

Patience is a lesson to be learned as I wait for the business transactions and taxi transport.

My American hurriedness has no value in this land where

relationships trump goals;
dancing trumps work;
time stands still; and
I am changed.

The Christmas Eve train from the beautiful aqua-painted Indian ocean of the refreshing coast of Mombasa turns into an unwelcome sauna treatment. I am not alone on my journey of waiting. Hundreds of international passengers clothed in saris, jeans, or traditional native dress join in the African song of acceptance, "Hakuna Matata."

Don't worry.

Hours pass waiting on the motionless train without any word or explanation. The swirling flies join their families in our carriage as we wait to know when our journey will end. At last the announcement arrives, and the wondering ceases. Derailment robbed us of our scheduled plans but blessed us with new relationships and a time for prayer.

Sunset and sunrise—another day and the squeak of the rusted wheels were back in motion. The train passes through the large city ghettos of cachexic, sick children to a place of healing green foliage deep in the shadow of Mount Kenya. The various creatures echo the diversity from the great, bold, thick-skinned elephants to the small, shy, sleek suni antelope. Together sharing the water hole, they reflect the diversity of the people of Africa. The playful monkeys call out their greetings to strangers, and the rain-filled rivers of looming Mount Kenya supply the water needs of the parched nation. A guided nature walk by an armed soldier through camouflaged green brush, roots, and nettles brings us to the place of rest.

A log for a chair and a rough, dark tree stump for a table contrasted with the shiny, white porcelain cup and saucer. In keeping with Kenya's British heritage, it is time for tea.

TIA. This is Africa.

January 5, 2013: The Quilt

The salty tears overflow from my eyes to scatter refreshment to the parched African soil. They represent the sweetness and pain of this day in a land on the other side of the world from "home." Sweet are the memories still very fresh in my mind, like a quilt of colors reflecting the travels with Serena, my "baby," through Kenya and Zambia. The darker patches of an unexpected layover in Ethiopia, and a greedy businesswoman in Kenya, pale in the light of the multicolored blessings that now dominate my thoughts. The diverse opportunities to learn the history of Kenya, love the orphans, and then swim with the dolphins and brightly colored fish are the earliest fabric of memories. Additional unique and precious swatches of cloth include the following:

We experienced warm white sand between our toes as we negotiated treasures with the traditional red-clad Maasai warriors on the aqua Indian Ocean.

A sun-filled morning journey in time to visit Mombasa's old town and Fort Jesus, with crimson-stained walls led by our Jesus-believing Muslim guide.

An international church visit was where we were the meaning of "international."

An afternoon journey in a glorified golf cart through the chaotic, packed city streets with the aroma of curry in our "takeaway" Indian cuisine on my lap. This experience will join the snapshots of my memory.

Christmas morning church service began with the greetings of "Merry Christmas" in a multitude of languages to remind us that soon there will be those from every tribe, nation, and tongue around the throne with us in worship. The very reason Jesus came. The day ended with the ultimate supply of gourmet, gluten-free food at Serena's namesake lodge. A good reminder to us that our tongues have not tasted all that God has prepared for us in heaven.

An AK 47–clad soldier led the walk in the medicinal Mount Kenya jungle that ended in a tea party and elephant bones! TIA.

Relaxing hours to gaze upon the cape buffalo, skype monkeys, suni antelope, and water buck (deer) as they hung out at the water hole, come rain or shine.

A return to Nairobi where the brown and white giraffes with their black, antibacterial-coated tongues are fed by visitors. Nine years previously, at that same feeding center, Serena, as a ten-year-old, had put a morsel of giraffe food in her own mouth after attempting to feed the animals! Needless to say, as her mother, I was happy to find out that giraffes do not actually transfer bacteria with their tongues!

Meetings with multiple Kenyan missionaries—hearing of their tales of tragedy and triumph brought inspiration to press on. This earth is not the way it was designed by our good heavenly Father; evil abounds and innocent bystanders feel the impact.

The Kijabe hospital visit brought the contrasting colors—brightness of hearing good news and darkness of telling bad news—and confirmed that we were there by Divine appointment.

Buses that begin with a sermon on Mondays brought lots of spiritual food for the day.

Missionaries at Zimba Hospital filled our eyes with flashes of colorful needs and possibilities for tomorrow.

January 1, 2013

Experiencing the drenching "smoke and thunder" mist of Victoria Falls producing ten thousand liters per second could not compare to the refreshment that came from sharing the Good News with a small group of men. They were more eager to share the meaning of the multi-colored bracelet—black represented the darkness of sin, those rebellious choices against God's will that we make; red represented the blood of Jesus that would pay the price for the sin each of us have committed; white represented the purity of heart that comes and the right relationship with God when we accept the sacrifice of Jesus; yellow represented the golden streets of heaven and all the other promises we have to live each day of our lives; and lastly, green was a reminder of the need to grow spiritually through reading the Bible, attending church, and talking with other believers. This man would prefer to tell this good news to the surrounding villagers rather than to make another sale that day. He rushed off to his home village to share the good news! Truly the best way to start the New Year!

Nshema (a traditional Zambian cuisine of cornmeal mush) was eaten with our hands, while we tried to avoid being burned by the temperature inside of the round white balls. After the meal, we went frolicking in the swimming pool in December, Zambia's hot season, which brought lots of laughter to us and the locals!

Zambia had a surplus of flies, crawling black centipedes, and ripe orange mangoes. All of them arrived daily at my doorstep to annoy, surprise, and delight me…in that order!

Alas, the memory-making with Serena came to an end, and I stood on the airport stairway for a final tear-blurred view of my loving daughter, who would return to the United States without me. The intense emotions spilled out of the container of my soul. I was overwhelmed with gratefulness and pride as I gazed at the woman of God she had become; however, my heart was truly broken as the splintered fork in the road became apparent. The moment had come, and each of us chose our divergent paths following the Creator in our own ways. The heart-shaped fabric we shared was torn asunder. I had only a hope and prayer that I would hug her again that year, so I gave her a parting triple-embrace dose. As Abraham did thousands of years ago, I placed my child on the altar of surrender. I would trust the Lord to provide the care for this young woman in her college years.

That bitter sight of her disappearing through the customs doors needed no photo. It will forever be lodged in my memory. I now sit alone, listening to the ticking of the clock, and know she is boarding the wide-bodied airplane. Soon she will leave African soil to plant her own seeds and bear the colorful fruit of her own God-given dreams in America. Her education, job, and marriage.

As I wait for the fruition of my own personal journey, I sew the quilted pieces of memory together to dry my tears and mend my bleeding heart. I will trust the Healer to join us together again with more sweet memories to share.

February 7, 2013: Living between the Mangoes and the Avocados

On my arrival in Zambia, the delicious, dripping sweet goodness of mangoes dropped from the tree in the garden and rolled up to my doorstep. I used my creative culinary arts to add them to salads, hot cereal, and drinks. It was my daily "manna from heaven" that I often ate at least three or four times, from sunrise to sunset. That was January, but now it is February. The mango trees have stopped dropping their fruit, and though the avocado tree is full, the fruit is still light green and hard. Similarly, the honeymoon of life in Zambia is over, and the hard day-in and day-out work has rooted me in reality.

Developing curriculum, teaching and demonstrating clinical skills, training more advanced students to function as assistants, while simultaneously delivering educational lectures and labs for the ninety-six novice students has been like I have been running a series of sprints. Monitoring professionalism in attendance, attitude, physical exam, and written documentation skills leaves me out of breath and exhausted by the evening hours. I await the fruit of my labors. The hard, green fruit is hanging in full view, but the season has not come...but with one more whiff...is that a scent of guacamole in the air?

As I wait in this season between two fruit trees, I find myself locked in. Literally locked between my office and the outside world, separated by a metal gate. Unknowingly, the keeper of the keys proceeded to lock the building doors without checking the offices, and so I sit, waiting to be freed to walk the paths of sunlight once again. If only I had quit work by 5:00 p.m. when others left for the day, I would not find myself at 5:15 p.m. relating to all the incarcerated people in the world! Those, like myself, living between a rock and a hard place.

Alas, my pleas for help have been heeded! Two unknown students approach and listen to my saga. Prompted by an unseen force, they mobilize into action, and with a few calls, I find myself connected to the keeper of the keys who assures me she will send her taxi to me with the desired key to release me from my jail time.

As the sun begins to set, a tall, dark man approaches the gate, and with a quick turn of the shiny gold key, he releases me from my prison. His requested payment for his effort...fifty kwacha (or five dollars). Freedom is not free, and I must pay to walk free from my "bondage" in the last remaining rays of this day. Somehow it feels like salt in the wound.

I take a moment to reflect on another freedom I experienced just a few days ago. Those academic assistants, still student physicians themselves, were like the avocado tree bearing its hard, green fruit. The regular watering and fertilizing I had done in their lives, preparing them to be assistants through special classes, handouts, time, and attention, had finally paid off. I watched them teach their younger colleagues in various clinical skills, and I was free to have a bite for lunch. I think the green fruit of March has just become a little riper!

February 14, 2013: The Disastrous Valentine's Day

Pink and red heart-shaped candy boxes filled with overflowing decadence is often what comes to mind with the mention of Valentine's Day. I have a multitude of diverse and colorful memories as I reflect back on a variety of over fifty Valentine Days to choose from, ranging from the darkest of colors to the sweetest of flavors. Just like with the beautifully displayed box of candies, I cannot pick my favorite!

One of the earliest memories of February 14 is of when I was about seven years old, and I had worn my chiffon red dress to the school party—with little white polka dots, white socks with lacy ruffles, and black patent shoes. I remember spinning and watching my dress float about me. It was a day filled with love and with laughter. Surely life was at its best.

As I entered the world of adulthood, I discovered my passion for the bright blue skies and white puffy clouds of Southern California. Thanks to my good friend, I had been prepared as a pilot. I had spent hours learning to navigate those clouds and to minimize the jolts of the landings. After months of training, the long-awaited day, February 14, 1983, had arrived and my flight instructor had determined I was ready for my solo flight.

Flying alone! The two-seat Cessna 152 was now quite a bit lighter without my instructor, who watched with trepidation from the taxi ramp as I was cleared to take off by the air traffic controller. Climbing into the clear royal-blue skies—two hundred, four hundred, eight hundred feet clicked by, and I continued to pull back on the wheel. I watched the altimeter soar along with my heart. My emotions were like caramel, nuts, and milk chocolate all mixed together as I tipped my wings to the world below. So fearful, yet overjoyed for this moment in time. The sun was beginning to set as I turned for the final approach, and my breath was snatched away as I heard the all-too-romantic words from the air traffic controller: "Seven-seven-six Romeo Juliet cleared to land." It was followed by a chuckle. The landing was definitely hard, but both the plane and I remained intact. What shook me up the most, though, was the supernatural arrangement that Valentine's Day—the identifying registration number for the plane I flew just happened to be 776RJ! It was like a delightful heavenly gift of chocolate frosting on a perfectly good cupcake of a day. I did not think life could get any better!

As the years passed, I found myself engaged and desiring to marry on that day of love. In a series of amazing twists, turns, and surprises, like white swirls on the tops of chocolates, the desires of my heart were granted. It was on reading my wedding card from my dear friend, Rose, that I first became aware of the story of Valentine's Day. The life of martyred Saint Valentinus became so real as I envisioned him spending his final hours encouraging a jailer's blind daughter, Julia, with education and visual imagery about the world she had never been gifted to see. His crime was that of marrying a Christian during Roman rule, when laws were instituted that made this God-ordained covenant illegal. As the story goes, the moment he perished in the jaws of the lions, Julia miraculously could see and later read his last note to his "dear Julia," which was signed, "Your Valentine."

As the first-year wedding anniversary approached, there was a greater expectation growing within my womb. My first-born daughter was being knitted together, and it was on the divinely scheduled ultrasound appointment on February 14, 1989, that I heard her heart beat for the first time and experienced love at first sight. The deep, rich, chocolate-like goodness of that day has been with me long after the flowers had faded.

The years have sped by, and I am smiling once again as I reflect on all the "home room" Valentine parties. As one of the suppliers of the sweets, I participated in the celebration activities with my girls during their elementary school years. The uniquely designed Valentine boxes graced each desk, and the excitement of a day filled with heart-shaped candies caused the children to squeal as they read each Valentine greeting from their classmate friends. Pink construction-paper hearts of all sizes were everywhere with white doilies and bright red punch for accent. The video of the story of St. Valentine was also a part of the celebration. There were also the memories of our family, but it was always hard to hear over the joyful laughter of the day.

The years passed, and my girls grew into two beautiful young ladies in their middle-school and high-school years, building more traditions. Valentine's evenings were filled with the succulent aroma of a well-cooked steak in the oven, music filling the air, and a dinner table dressed with all the family's finest china, glassware, and napkins. We would have time to reflect on the loving couples we knew and finish off the evening time with prayers for the men the Lord was raising up as future husbands for my young ladies.

Today was a very different Valentine's Day, and I can't describe it any other way than simply disastrous. There were no red hearts or boxes of chocolates. No roses scenting the air or beautiful music prompting the feet to dance. It was the unexpected flavor in the bite that initially left me wanting for a different choice. As the flavor of the day absorbed, I realized it could have been one of my favorites after all.

I am six weeks into fulfilling my divine call as the only emergency medicine trained physician/professor in the country of Zambia. I find my days filled with opportunities to participate in this developing country's growing pains. Without a coordinated EMS system, the country just completed their three days of national grieving for the single greatest loss of human life in their history. The bus accident and subsequent lack of coordinated emergency services resulted in the loss of over fifty-four lives.

My heart grieves for the families who lost the love of their lives. It pains me that some could have been granted another Valentine's Day with advanced preparation and training on many levels.

Today I joined over twenty strategic leaders of Zambia representing a wide variety of skills. I always believed that love is a verb. During this day, I saw the melding of many passionate people working together for the sake of others. Through various meetings we reviewed the drafted disaster plans for the government hospital. Soon they would have a practice disaster, a fire drill to prepare people and prevent further loss of life. I also spent time with the volunteer emergency responders, longing to learn more to save people. Gratefully, I gave the gift I had for the day, God's love and teaching about irregular heart rhythm recognition.

At the close of this Valentine's Day, yet one more minor disaster needed mending. My fourteen-year-old friend Andrew experienced an unexpected ripping of his leg flesh on a sharp, shiny metal object and helplessly watched as heart-pumped blood leaked out the flap-shaped hole. The novelty of the event soon wore off, and various layers of anatomy boldly shouted to be placed back under cover. As with love, some things are best left unseen and unheard. Love covers a multitude of sins, and so layers of anatomy cover what is best not to be shared with the outside world. With some years of experience, a brown wooden coffee table, and lots of improvisation, I went to work. Substituting a local anesthetic option, family members encouraging him to "bite the bullet," and a few quick stitches using very thick suture material, I found my day coming to a close in the shape of a V on an adolescent leg! Could life get any better than this?

March 10, 2013: Raining on the Inside

It started with just a drop. Next, there was a small running stream falling from above the large wooden pulpit, accompanied by a few whispers. The thunder was roaring outside, and soon a wall fountain suddenly appeared before my eyes. Though a fascinating sight, it was a bit disturbing to the preacher, who stepped back, arms flailing, and let the men move the podium back, rearrange the brightly colored flowers, move the paisley-printed tithing bags, and reposition the microphones out of direct line of the uninvited steady-flowing faucet. Last but not least, the communion table found a new resting place to prevent soggy bread later. Pools of water drained down to greet the first rows of parishioners, marking out unusual distracting patterns as they flowed.

The preacher hardly missed a beat, as if this was a usual Sunday occurrence, and picked right up with his message, "The Judgment of God."

I have attended church for about forty years, and this was a first. Surely, I have heard many sermons on various subjects, complete with "stage effects," from the comforting harp music during the reading of the Twenty-Third Psalm to the painful retelling of the great suffering and sacrifice of Jesus, complete with the pounding of nails in the background. Never a flowing wall fountain and damp toes mixed with fire and brimstone. I would have preferred the sermon about Noah and the ark or even Jonah and the whale. Then the aha moment came. A verse so dear to me, Matthew 28:19–20, stressing "go to all the nations," concludes, "and lo I am with you always, even unto the end of the world." My God has a sense of humor, and I can accept the joy in this new home. Live and learn. TIA. This is Africa!

March 13, 2013: Living in a Broken World

The man with the broken leg navigates the broken staircase with the broken wooden crutch because of the broken elevator at the broken-down hospital.

I know brokenness is not just an African phenomenon, but somehow, it is just magnified here, where so many systems have stopped working years ago, yet people continue, day in and day out, moving in their halting way to their final destination.

What can I do?

As the women sit outside the medical ward, weeping over the death of a son, caused by malaria that broke his blood cells, they, too, are broken. I stop, sit, and pray with them and offer the only comforting words I know to give. I have come to help students become better doctors. I remind them of the pain that Mary felt as she looked upon the broken body of her son, Jesus, hanging on a cross. As his final act of love on earth, he bridged the lives of his disciple John and Mary, providing lifelong comfort for his mother by this disciple of love, John. Jesus paved the way for that same brokenhearted woman to see her beloved son and Savior for all eternity in His perfect, unbroken world.

Hope is restored, our tears dry, and peace returns in the midst of a broken world.

March 15, 2013: Oh, Shining Star

Brilliant in the darkness. The silent "prophet" pointing toward the newborn Jesus, the Light of the world. Hovering closer to the infant Creator than any other star dared to go. Shedding the glow that would draw others to the King of Kings, where the three royal kings could fulfill their call, to fall on their knees and worship.

The star named by its Creator before the beginning of earthly time. What was the name you were given?

Oh, that I might be an earthly star bringing the Light of hope to a dark world filled with seeking travelers! In my silent obedience, others will be drawn to worship Him.

March 20, 2013: Look at the Birds!

The morning dawns in all its glory with the chirps, crows, chatters, and cock-a-doodle-doos. As I step out on my morning journey from my fenced-in suburban home, I hear them and I see them.

They are silent vibrant yellow-breasted finches in the camouflaged green foliage.

They are the milk-chocolate-brown sparrows in the heavily laden avocado trees.

They are the proud black-and-white tuxedo crows declaring their turf.

They are the flaming red-topped roosters screaming out that another day has begun.

So different, yet with the shared skill of reminding me of a daily truth and the words of my Creator:

> Look at the birds of the air; they do not sow or reap or store away in barns, and yet your heavenly Father feeds them. Are you not much more valuable than they? (Matt. 6:26, NIV)

As I continue on my day's journey, the chirps, crows, chatter, and cock-a-doodle-doos are replaced by the rumble of cars, the rattle of buses, and the tooting of horns. Distracted by the sounds around me, I have become deaf to the calls of the birds. The busyness of life has replaced the quiet stillness. My heart becomes fearful and my vision is impaired. As I purpose to make the turn and head for home, I once again begin to hear the chirps, crows, and chatters, and they remind me of His words: "Be still and know that I am God, I will be exalted in the nations, I will be exalted in the earth" (Ps. 46:10, NIV).

March 21, 2103: Driven by Luck

Green shamrocks and the rolling hills of Ireland come to mind with the "luck of the Irish." "Best of luck" and "I wish you luck" are common phrases in the United States but always something that just did not sit right with me. What does "luck" have to do with a well-orchestrated plan of God? There are no coincidences, just God instances—times when He prefers to be anonymous. But now I can officially say I am driven by Luck. My new driver, Simwanza Luck, goes by the nickname of "Lucky," because he almost died about the time of his birth. He has taught me "*Mulunguu Amadalasay*." God bless you. He has developed my interest in the names of Africa.

As a teacher of ninety-six students, I had the challenge to know my students by name during the short eight-week course. I was successful with some but not all; the easy ones like Precious, John, Nathan, Sarah, and Natasha were like a breath of fresh air while I still found myself struggling with Mulenga Mainza, Chisanga Katepa, Fiseko Kampamba, and Lungwebungu Mwenya and wondering what was the first and last name and their gender. One female student was Chifuntu, Sampa not to be confused with the male Sampa, Brian. (Sometimes *Sampa* can be a last name and sometimes it can be a first name—probably like our version of Allen.) Then there were the seven Phiris: Jackson, Titus, Emmanuel, Evans, Caleb, Arnold, and Walaza. It was like Smith in the United States. Then there were the Indian students like Shahin Saifurrahman. As my head was still swirling with their names, I realized I was getting new names. I became everyone's "auntie," "momma," "mommie," or "prof." I guess with all the confusion that can abound, Lucky was lucky to have a very simple name.

March 23, 2013: When Left is Right

Black and white; wrong and right.

I have been described as rigid and dogmatic in my beliefs, and at times, I certainly would have to agree. My core values that have developed during well over a half century are immovable. I would like to think that in many other areas I am more flexible and adjustable as I near my completion of three months of flexibility on African soil. I have learned to view life through the eyes of an African, think as they might think, and make decisions as they might decide. Today, as I sat behind the wheel of a car in Africa, I learned that right is wrong, and what seems wrong is really right.

As a country under British influence for years, Zambia adopted their system of the rules of the road, and drivers were taught the left side of the road is the right place to turn your wheels. Something deep within my being resists this foreign way. My eyes have become accustomed to seeing it, my legs to walking on the left side of a crowd ascending or descending stairs, and experientially I have accepted the flow of traffic from the view of a front-seat passenger on the left side of the vehicle without any more adrenaline surges for me or the driver.

Driving was different.

As I positioned myself behind the wheel on the right side of my newly purchased car, turned on the ignition of the silver '90s Toyota Corolla, and advanced into the residential street, my years as a US driver took over the controls, and I found myself meandering on the right side of the road. Alarmed, my passenger alerted me and redirected me to the "right side" or left side of the road. Without oncoming traffic to contend with, my life was spared, and so was his—this time.

Watch out, Africa!

March 30, 2013: Easter Weekend: Living between Friday and Sunday

Thud…thud…thud…the pounding of nails still echoes in my mind as the Roman guards crucified my Savior. The blood-drenched wood is still the visual reminder of yesterday. All my yesterdays, when hopes were snuffed out, dreams died, and life lost its meaning. He was the long-awaited Christ, our Redeemer, the Hope for all humankind. How could I live without Him?

How could this happen—did the creation really just kill the Creator?

On this Saturday of living in the shadow of the cross, I join with the followers of Jesus from two thousand years ago, hiding in their disillusioned thoughts. Our friend, Lord, and Savior, is dead. The blind will remain in darkness, and the deaf will live in silence.

No more miracles of fish and bread on grassy hills.

No more calming of the hostile, drenching storms.

No more freedom for those in ironclad bondage to demons and death.

No more laughter, only tears.

Tearstained faces join me and the multitude of his disciples. Linda and Joyce, my dear friends, grieve their first Easter weekend without their husbands. This side of heaven, death still has a sting as they are living the loneliness between Friday and Sunday, between the power of death and the power of the resurrection. It is a very cold, darkly shrouded tomb in which they wait in their night watch.

Sunday morning breaks the chains of death. Look now! The Son has risen, and Jesus shines now like a beacon in the night, calling you to look toward the resurrection hope.

Dear friends, fix your eyes on the hope only Jesus can give as an anchor for your soul in these storm-tossed waters of life. The hope realized in that Sunday dawn breaks forth again and again into our lives. Life and hope are birthed beyond the shadow of the cross.

Hope that He will come again.

Hope that He will dry our tears and make all things right.

Hope that He will once again ignite our dreams for tomorrow.

March 31, 2013: Resurrected Words on Easter Sunday

Jesus's first words after his resurrection were questions in times of sadness and loss:

"Woman, why are you crying?"—Death has lost its victory.

"Who are you looking for?"—Dry your tears and you will see Me clearly.

Then He calls us by name. He comes in our fears as we hide from our enemies and says, "Peace be with you."

"Receive the Holy Spirit."

"Forgive."

He comes in our doubts and says, "Peace be with you."

"Reach out your hand and put it into my side. Stop doubting and believe."

He comes in our failures and says, "Throw your net on the right side"—to encourage us to keep trying.

"Do you truly love me more than these?"—to remind us about true success.

"Follow me"—to know He will lead us with His presence; we will never be alone.

April 2, 2013: Tearstained White Coats

Under the azure-blue sky, the white contrast on green grass was a stark reminder of those unanswered questions that stand out in brilliance against the everyday routines. Education at the University of Zambia Medical School came to a halt today, finals were postponed, meetings delayed, and the air was somber. Medical students clad in their symbol of healing sat helplessly and wondered "Why?" Some things in life we will never understand. Even professors, those who have invested their entire life explaining the *hows* and *whys* of the human body, were silenced.

Just when the finish line was in sight and the crowds were cheering, the racer drops silently, alone. Leonard was in his twenties, unknown to me but a familiar face for hundreds of fellow students and faculty. He was just weeks away from finishing the seven-year stretch of medical school. He was involved in soccer and loved by his family. No complaints or concerns. Somehow, sometime on Thursday evening, surrounded by books packed with knowledge of the human body, he laid his head down and breathed his last.

As the grieving father voiced his "whys?" the pain spilled over, and teardrops fell on well-worn white fabric throughout the memorial gathering. A soldier in the battle against human suffering has been lost, and the hopeful remaining class of fifty-nine presses on despite the paralyzing uncertainties that come from living in this world. Draped in tearstained white coats, they march onward.

United, they gather strength as the choir sings, "Take my life and let it be always, only for my King, take my hands and let them move at the impulse of thy love, at the impulse of thy love."

April 21, 2013: Stalking

It could have been an international crime scene investigation, with eyes straining for clues in the dark-green foliage and coded pieces of data collected in whispers. Experts in their field gathered together beneath the tree to debate the details of what they were seeing and hearing. They came from Holland, South Africa, Australia, the United Kingdom, the United States, Denmark, Ireland, Germany, Sweden, and of course, Zambia. They shared English with a variety of accents, but they also shared their own cryptic vocabulary. "Turuco," "weaver," and "white-helmet shriek" were common terms to them and a foreign language to me.

It was a sunny morning, and I was drawn to follow this band of twenty strangers headed into the bush. The path of green stalks of grass was of shoulder height, and the scattered bright-orange African daisies welcomed us into a world of beautiful sights and coded sounds. The vibrant yellow butterflies danced around the dark blue butterflies with the red-dotted margins.

Less than three kilometers from my home, I entered the world of birding for the first time. I came unprepared, without binoculars, which left me handicapped and dependent on others at times. In my naïvely blinded condition, I grew to appreciate the chirps, whistles, and songs of the creatures they had come to stalk. As a bright-green-bodied bird passes and waves its red-winged greeting, one member quick on the binocular draw makes the ID. "Turuco."

Next, the small fluttering wings of a group of three catch our attention, and one says "Weaver," another says, "Sun Bird," and the third says, "Honey Guide." Confusion in the ranks precedes the scramble through their packs to pull out their guidebooks. The drafted husband of one enthusiast positions his eleven-inch zoom lens: ready, aim—captured! The digital view settles the score, and all agree: "Honey Guide." One more dash of sweetness added to the list of sightings for the day.

Walking farther, we see more diversity. The soaring brown snake eagle circles alone up above, spreading his white-tipped wings for the world to see. The gang of white-helmet shriek shows off their black-and-white stripes as they pass by with a chatter, declaring their turf. In an effort to declare war, an experienced leader pulls out the big guns. A phone app is activated, and the bird call goes forth! From the other side of the woods, an echo is heard as the challenge is met. Closer and closer the chattering gang approaches again, circles, and leaves. No lives lost.

Though focused heavenward on this morning walk, I take a moment to enjoy my earthly surroundings. Lest they be outdone, the smaller creatures on the trail display their contrasting colors and talents. The one-inch black red-striped beetle, the "blister beetle," slowly mounts to the top of the stalk of green grass swinging in the breeze and launches into flight.

May 2, 2013: When the Poor Give to the Poor

Days pass, but the memories remain fresh. The five-day travels from the "big city" of Lusaka to the countryside of the town of Mkushi took only six hours, but the journey left an impact for eternity.

A mission trip within a mission trip for me. The team consisted of forty-three students of Lusaka, all in their twenties but representing dreams for diverse professions of medicine, dentistry, nursing, pharmacy, accounting, and environmental sciences. Together with the faith-filled hosts, we joined for one cause—that the people of Mkushi would know the love of Jesus better because we came. We left our comfort zone and primary languages of English and Nyanja for the land of the Bemba and Lala people.

Each morning before the break of day, the students gathered for prayer, calling upon the One who could break through the bondage of darkness that imprisoned those of this farming community. The tears flowed, and the songs brought hope and encouragement to us all.

The days were filled with teaching, prayers, and laughter. In the market-place, surrounded by piles of dried sardines and as many flies, we checked blood pressures and blood sugars and taught about malaria, HIV, hyperten-sion, and the precious blood sacrifice of Jesus. There were prayers offered to hospital patients and prisoners alike.

Smiles flashed, and laughter was common among the nearly one hundred orphans as we gave them a sweet cake, juice, and an encouraging hug. We danced the hokey-pokey together, and they taught me a few of their local games. They sat captivated by the story of Jesus's love, which was demonstrat-ed with a three-dimensional cube covered in pictures of his life. The children each shared their lofty dreams of the future.

I had the additional privilege to travel with my local guide, Edward, on a trek through tall grasses and hills to the village of the Lala people. A black snake slithered on the pathway ahead, and Edward reassured me it was not a poisonous variety. The local mineral springs brought water to the thirsty, growing tomatoes and other plants he was cultivating. Nearby, the women washed their clothes and dried them on the bushes. As we continued quietly for a few kilometers, the si-lence was suddenly broken with the excitement of the wrinkled grandma echoing, "La-la-la-la-la-la-la-la," her cultural expression of joy, prompted by a surprise visit by her grandson. Edward was returning after over one year in the big city. In this village, the old were suffering from malaria and sitting in the sun to warm their aching bones, and one gray-haired man seemed particularly uncomfortable that day. I offered up a prayer to warm his soul. The children were home from school because they could not afford the three dollars a month that it would have cost their parents to send them to school. Instead, they danced about barefoot, and the young mothers had babies wrapped around their backs. The young men carried slingshots on their head and hoped someday to capture something edible. They were all related. They gladly shared with us their grass-covered huts and a cup of cold water.

The star-filled nights were sprinkled with cheers and tears from those gathered to sit on the dirt to see the Jesus film in the Bemba language. The scattered break times were filled with music and local dancing. The shoeless and coatless thin children gathered around me as I spread out a yellow-and-brown-striped blanket to wrap them in the tangible love of Jesus. My heart was warmed in the process. Many, both young and old, made the decision to begin a spiritual journey that would change their destiny for eternity.

Spending time with the Lala people of Mkushi, Zambia.

May 20, 2013: After the Disaster

Bodies were strewn around the parking lot, vehicles nosed into one another, and plenty of screaming reverberated from every direction. As the disaster drill began, our actors and actresses were well rehearsed for this final exam, only they were not the ones being tested. After a week of conference teaching, the Emergency Response Center and Levy Mwanawasa Hospital staff knew the importance of prioritizing patients based on injury, and it was time for the shouts for help to begin as my team evaluated the care provided. As the red lights flashed and sirens blared, the ambulances responded to the scene of the three-car collision with fifteen victims. Real adrenaline was flowing amid the pooling fake blood around amputated limbs. As the emergency medical technicians quickly entered the stage of this unfolding drama, they began to sort out patients followed by conducting rapid lifesaving interventions.

The tagged "red" patients required emergency treatment or they would die. The "black" patients were already dead and were without hope of resuscitation or need for transfer. The "yellow" could swing either way without intervention soon, and the "green" patients could walk away with minor injuries or be recruited as extra hands. There were also bystanders and "family" members joining in the scene of chaos.

As the victims were transported to the back door of the hospital, the doctors and nurses sprang into action applying dressings, starting intravenous catheters, barking out orders, and starting cardiopulmonary resuscitation. News cameras were rolling and photos taken. Bodies were writhing now on the floor of the casualty department and spilling into the halls, given the significant shortage of beds.

Additional staff was recruited from other departments, but that left the remaining nurses forced to respond to their own internal disasters, such as patients having heart attacks or choking on an apple.

In the end, four people "died" but later resurrected, and all showed up for tea break—a new definition for success was birthed!

May 23, 2013: Home for Hippos and Elephants

Home is along the Zambezi River for many creatures large and small. As the river snakes its way through Zambia, it makes its dramatic "smoke and thunder" plunge at the Victoria Falls. David Livingstone named it after the Queen of Scotland, but the locals know it as "Mosi-o-Tunya." Upriver, it is quiet and a place of refreshment for the large gray pachyderms that travel across in a line of four, holding on to one another's tails with their trunks. At times, they lose their footing and begin to swim but still remain somehow in that amazing chain of elephants of all sizes.

The crocodile, in his prehistoric frozen state, lies in the sun along the marsh, waiting for an unsuspecting light-footed impala or clumsy warthog. The bee-eaters sit perched on the naked branches of a nearby tree like Christmas ornaments with their shimmering bright-green feather coats and bright-pink splashes of chest color.

In the stillness of the early-morning mist on the river's edge, a ripple appears and then another, followed by bubbles and black eyes. The hippo family of five are popping up and down as if playing a hide-and-seek game just ten feet from the river bank.

God's creativity shouts loudly in the silence!

MEDICAL TERMS

Arterial Blood Gas: test to determine pH, oxygen, and carbon dioxide levels in the blood and status of the respiratory efforts

Chest film: chest x-ray

CPR: cardiopulmonary resuscitation

Intubation: placement of a breathing tube to assist patients who are not able to breathe well enough on their own or are preparing for surgery

Integrative Medicine (functional medicine): holistic approach to patient care incorporating alternative and complimentary modalities to treat the physical, emotional, and spiritual dimensions

IV: intravenous catheter to administer fluids, blood, or medications

Large bore: large caliber allowing for greatest amount of fluids

MI (heart attack): oxygen and glucose supply is cut off from heart muscle, damaging cells and function

MRI: type of scan using magnetic resonance imaging that can clearly see different areas of anatomy

Scoop and Run: quickly place patient in the ambulance with very little resuscitation efforts on the scene to expedite treatment available at the hospital

STAT: immediately, without delay

Stroke: oxygen and glucose supply is cut off from brain tissue, damaging respective function

Tumor markers: blood-testing method of indirectly assessing the trend (decrease or increase) in cancerous tumors or metastasis used in conjunction with chemotherapeutic interventions

70482307R00080

Made in the USA
San Bernardino, CA
02 March 2018